Buddhism
Socialism
Marxism
Ambedkarism
Pratitya Samutpada

'Maha Mahopadhyaya'
B.S. RAMULU
Social Philosopher
BC Commission First Chairman, Telangana State

ALL RIGHTS RESERVED

All rights reserved. No part of this publication may be reproduced, stored in or introduced into a retrieval system, or transmitted, in any form by any means may it be electronically, mechanical, optical, chemical, manual, photocopying, or recording without prior written permission of the Publisher/ Author.

Buddhism
Socialism
Marxism
Ambedkarism
Pratitya Samutpada
By
B.S. Ramulu

Ph: +91 8331966987

Copy Right: **B.S. Ramulu**
First Edition: 2023

Published By: Kasturi Vijayam
Published on: April,2024

ISBN (Paperback): 978-81-969150-2-5

Print On Demand

Ph:0091-9515054998
Email: Kasturivijayam@gmail.com
Book Available
@
Amazon(Worldwide), flipkart

DEDICATED TO

The great personalities changed the human history, into the Common man's perspective with reasoning and hoisted the flag of native people's self respect.

Charvakas

Buddha

Kabir Das

Guru Ravidas

Pothuluri Virabhramham

Mahathma Jyothibha Phuley

Savithribhai Phuley

Sahu Maharaj

Marx, Engels

Gramsi, Georgie Lucas

Periyar Ramaswamy

Narayana Guru

Dr. B.R. Ambedkar

Ram Manohar Lohiya

Simon Debower

B.P. Mandal...

Inspired by the guidelines and their Historical Contribution

B.S. RAMULU
Social Philosopher

Contents

Dr. E. Venkatesu x
Dr. K. S. Chalam xv
Dr. Katti Padma Rao xix
Dr.G.R. Krishna Gogineni xxiv
Dr. Bharat Patankar xxvi

1. Buddhism Socialism 1
2. Marxism Socialism 38
3. Ambedkarism Socialism 74
4. Dr. B.R. Ambedkar - Economist 85
5. Pratitya Samutpada 97
   Profile of the Author 117

Acknowledgements

I Acknowledge the services rendered by the eminent personalities to change the society and inspire many, who think of the society of a downtrodden, like Dr. K.S. Chalam,, former VC and UPSC Member; Prof. E. Venkatesu, Dept. of Political Science, Dr. Bharat Patankar, Eminent Thinker, and activist; Dr. G.R. Krishna Gogineni, Prof. of Eminence, Maha Kavi ,Dr. Katti Padma Rao, Social Philosopher,

To the Editors of 'Dalith Voice', 'Edureetha', Ekalavya', 'Gabbilam', 'Samanthara', 'Buddha Bhoomi', Monthly Magazines Which have published several times.

To the friends and readers who have been supporting since 35 years...

To the teachers who taught this philosophy in their training classes...

To the United front Dalit (OBC, SC, ST) writers, artists, and intellectuals who inspired... and colleagues Guda Anjaiah, U. Sambasivarao, V.G.R. Naragoni, Mastarjee, Ingilala Ramachandra Rao Bodhi, Jupalli Satyanarayana, Dr. Nanumasa Swamy, K. Sita Ramulu, Dr. Jaya Salomi, Anisheti Rajitha, Khader Mohiuddin, M. Ananthaiah, Durgam Subbarao, B.M. Leelakumari, J.S. Raghupathi Rao, K. Rama Laxman, P. Ramulu, P.N. Prasangi, G.R. Kurme, Dr. Damera Ramulu and other colleagues...

To K.K. Raja of Lata Raja Foundation who published the first edition of this book...

I heartily thank Mr. K.G.M. Prasad, Ex Service man; The translator and A. Gavarraju, Bahujan Activist.

Last but not least, I have to display gratitude and love to the co-operation extended by my family members, our family mentor and my wife Mrs. Shymala and my children, who beard all the hurdles patiently, they faced in their life, to see my success of what I am today. I'm not what I'm at present, unless I have the support of whole family, without any expectations. There are no words to match their sacrifice, to make me stand as the writer, philosopher and crusader of the downtrodden.

PREAMBLE

Dr. B.R. Ambedkar was the Chairman of the Indian Constitution Drafting Committee, and the Constitution of India, which began with a Preamble or Preamble. Many aspects of the Objectives Resolution introduced by Jawaharlal Nehru in the Constituent Assembly are missing in this. It can be said that the philosophical foundations of the Constitution lie in this Preamble. After the 42nd Constitutional Amendment Act, 1976 the Preamble to the Constitution reads as follows.

THE CONSTITUTION OF INDIA
PREAMBLE

WE, THE PEOPLE OF INDIA, having solemnly resolved to constitute India into a **[SOVEREIGN, SOCIALIST SECULAR DEMOCRATIC REPUBLIC]** and to secure to all its citizens:

JUSTICE Social, economic, and political.

LIBERTY of thought, expression, belief, faith, and worship.

EQUALITY of status and of opportunity; and to promote among them all.

FRATERNITY assuring the dignity of the individual and the [unity and integrity of the Nation];

IN OUR CONSTITUENT ASSEMBLY this twenty-sixth day of November 1949 do **HEREBY ADOPT, ENACT AND GIVE TO OURSELVES THIS CONSTITUTION.**

---

1. Subs by the Constitution (Forty-second Amendment) Act, 1976, Sec 2, for "Sovereign Democratic Republic" (w.e.f.3.1.1977)

2. Subs, by the Constitution (Forty-second Amendment) Act, 1976, Sec 2. for "Unity of the Nation" (we.f.3.1.1977)

Let's look at the proportion of people's representatives in many countries of the world.

1.	In China	2980
2.	India	543+245
3.	U.K	650+793
4.	Italy	630+321
5.	Germany	709+69
6.	Japan	465+242
7.	Russia	450+168
8.	America	435+100

When viewed in terms of population ratio. Compared to China, USA, UK, Germany and Russia... India should have 2650 members in Parliament. Then only the people will get proper representation. Now even a fourth of it is not represented. We need to increase our seats four or five times when compared to other countries. Today's running democracy is becoming a public domain that is not available to the people. Therefore, when compared to America, China, and England, the number of members in the Parliament in India should increase four and a half times and also in the state legislatures, the number of members should increase four times. According to the population, there is one member of parliament for every 97 thousand people in London. India has one member of Parliament for every 658,000 people. Notice how much difference there is. How can democracy be accessible to the people when this is the case? The solution is to increase representation.

A social philosopher who pioneered a new way of thinking

- Professor E. Venkatesu
Department of Political Science,
Central University of Hyderabad

A well-known author, social philosopher, and known for objective assessment of an individual or an organization is none other than BS Ramulu (BSR). He was the chairman of Telangana State First Backward Classes Commission. In my view, it is a historical opportunity to write the foreword to the book "Buddhism - Socialism, Marxism - Ambedkarism" written by BSR.

I was for a long period of time a distant reader of BSR's writings, however, in close contact with him for the past few years. As we come closer, I was a regular reader of his writings and in the process, I learned a lot from his way of writing and experiences. It would be appropriate to illustrate a few events as evidence of closeness.

Until 2004, my acquaintance with BSR was reading his works, listening to his lectures, and having an opportunity to be a co-speaker in some of the meetings and conferences. Till 2004, I wrote about 100 articles in Telugu and some of them are published with the title "Democracy and Development-A Backward Classes Perspective" on behalf of Vishalasahiti, which is being managed by BSR. The book has got very well recognition in Telugu states and subsequently led to the intensification of the voice of BCs.

BSR also attended the open viva of My PhD thesis on 'Social Deprivation and Social Mobilization'A Case Study of Backward Classes in Andhra Pradesh in the Department of Political Science at Hyderabad Central University in August 2004 as a participant. Noted political scientist and human rights activist Prof. G. Haragopal was supervisor for my PhD and external examiner was Prof. Manoranjan

Mohanthy of Delhi University. Coming together of these three stalwarts such as Prof. G. Haragopal, Prof. Mohanthy and BSR it was an occasion to recollect their experiences of the Naxalite movement since the 1970s. Prof. Manoranjan Mahanthy revealed that they were arrested and put in the police station at "Indravelli". They shared their historic experiences with the students for a while.

After the formation of the Telangana State in 2014, BSR was the First Chairman of the State BC Commission. He used to invite me as a resource person and to speak as a subject expert in the conferences organized to identify the BC castes. During the conferences and workshops, I suggested adopting the methodology of 'Putting the last first' and "Most Backward must get the First priority in the allocation of resources. BSR as chairman of the Commission gave serious thought and considered them in the recommendations.

With this brief intimacy with BSR, now let me come to discuss the importance of political ideas. Due to a lack of historical knowledge, many people believe that the origin of political ideas, and philosophy are traced out to only Ancient Greek and Western countries. The main reason for this state of condition is not making deeper attempts into political thought and ideas in the vernacular languages. Such an impression is predominantly reflected in English-language writings that reject the political thought and ideas, which have been existing in the non-West world. However, BSR is making such an effort to fill the gap, while illustrating Indian tradition itself as a potential source for tracing out indigenous ideas and thoughts, philosophy and writing them in Telugu. The writings in the mother tongue will be a basis for questioning the dominance of their own existence and ideas instead of borrowed ideas.

With this purpose, the book is brought out. The first chapter of the book is on "Buddhism-Socialism" which deals with the idea that the notion of socialism is not necessarily a Western concept but it has been injected into the minds of the people right from childhood days through the textbooks. Therefore, BSR emphasizes to clear about the concept in terms of tracing out the historical genesis of the idea of socialism. That is why one must read the book to understand that the concept of socialism has got roots in this country itself. It is a concept that was born and grown in India itself right from the Buddhist tradition. But due to the lack of knowledge, the Communists in the country set aside Buddhism and glorified Karl Marx, Engels, Lenin, and Mao. The reason for the false consciousness about Buddhist socialist thought among the communists is that they strongly believe in the orthodox idea that 'Religion is the opium of the people'. But they miserably failed in understanding that Buddhism is not a religion. Religion is built on mythology, but Buddhism has been a historical reality.

I often say to my students in the classroom that in this country, a person, who never saw the Communist Manifesto is doing left-wing politics, a person, who never touched cow dung is doing Hindutva politics and a person who has not read Mahatma Gandhi's autobiography is preoccupying with the centrist politics. However, BSR does not belong to such a group and he never criticizes or writes without reading substantial evidence. That is why he studied Marxism for several decades before criticizing Marxism from an Indian perspective. In his writings on Marxism, BRS, essentially touch the foundation of philosophical roots and historical background, contributing to the social transformation and critical aspect. Therefore, BRS writings can be understood even by a common man. He has been following DD Kosambi methodology, which applied Marxism to understand the history of India.

The assessment of BSR about the Communists in the country from the 1950s to 1980, criticized Ambedkar as a revisionist, British, and Congress agent. Therefore, multifaceted genius Ambedkar and his ideas have been alienated from the ideological, political, economic, and social discourse in the country. However, Karamchedu incident in the 1980s and Chunduru in the 1990s brought Ambedkar to light once again. As a result, since the 1980s, the social thinkers such as U. Sambasiva Rao and Kancha Ilaiah from non-parliamentary left parties brought back the question of caste in India. Subsequently, Muralidhar Rao Commission, which was announced to implement the reservations for BCs in Andhra Pradesh, and the Mandal movement at the national level focused on Ambedkar's ideology. The revival process was resulted in the weakening of the Parliamentary left. In the 1990s onwards Ambedkarism was revived and intensified the movement for asserting the rights and identities in the country.

Right from the beginning of the New Millennium (year 2000), Ambedkarism attracted scholars, intellectuals, thinkers, and researchers inside and outside the country. International organizations such as the United Nations declared Ambedkar's birthday as "Knowledge Day". Both central and state governments started providing overseas scholarships for their studies on Ambedkar. The Maharashtra government purchased a house, where Ambedkar used to live in London for his higher studies.

In the changed context, to revive the left parties once again put forward the slogan of "Lal-Neel" (Left and Blue) i.e., Marxism and Ambedkarism to retain their presence in the politics of India. It is in this context BSR emphasized the need for the historical necessity of coming together of the leftists and Ambedkarities. The idea of coming together of the two ideological streams, which are committed to the cause of the historically deprived social groups, is an alternative ideological front. However, the question is how far "Leftism - Ambedkarism" will move together is a matter for the future to decide. Therefore, BSR also suggests that both of them cherish the ideological legacy of Buddha, Ambedkar and Periyar Ramaswami and Karl Marx towards building a casteless and classless society in India. The proposition of BSR is new and futuristic. The proposition in the book is a thought-provoking exercise and it has got contemporary relevance.

But the issue is whether the present generation is having the habit of reading a hard copy of a book. Most of people nowadays, read books and other stuff on their mobiles, laptops computers, and kindle. Therefore, keeping in view the changed situation, BSR must also make a book to be available online, so that it will reach more readers. As a result, not only Telugu people spread all over the world will update themselves about the new ideas in Telugu states but also the book will serve as a bridge for those who have similar ideas and bring them to a common ground.

Two words

- Acharya K. S. Chalam
Visakhapatnam

Buddhism - Socialism - Marxism - Ambedkarism book authored by B.S. Ramulu is being reprinted at the right time. We are aware that some chapters of this book have been published in the past and have led to extensive discussion. Common readers know that the doubts and fears raised by Ramulu about three decades ago are now turned mostly correct. Some of its philosophical, practical, understanding and theoretical discussions are not as easily understood by ordinary people as they are understood by activists and activists. But let's suppose that in the current situation of the country, every citizen is in a position to understand these in the form of daily problems that he has taken as his own life. They all need to be understood in the correct perspective. A platform for a theoretical basis for that has to be started somewhere. There is now a good social environment in the Telugu states in the form of Dalit, Bahujan and democratic movements. But, what is to be done? Activists have doubts about how to build it. That is why many types of organizations and movements have been formed as multiple platforms. In order to convert all these into one or two mainstream movements, the necessary basis for such a change should be on social, economic and cultural aspects. Those who believe in democracy such as political parties, associations and organizations can be formed as a group. But if they interfere with each other, the purpose for which a forum anticipated will be defeated! What then? A theory will have to wait and see it is practiced. The social awakening started with Buddha in our country's history, and it is continued as Ambedkar's legacy in contemporary society, is grasped by only few. Ramulu has explained these things in this book.

The Arya Anarya issue has resurfaced in the last decade after the Dravidian roots were found in archeological excavations and the results of DNA research came out to prove the continuation of the Indus River Civilization up to Vaigai River region of Tamil Nadu in the area called 'Keeladi' are the same. A solution was found to the problem raised by Mahatma JyotiRaoPhule, but the government that came to power at the center did not like it, especially their intelligentsia. Therefore, immediately after the discoveries of Dravidian roots of India, the ruling class started showing evidence that the Saraswati civilization had its roots in Uttar Pradesh through some archaeological excavations, to say that Arya Brahmins are from here. There are others who say that there is no Arya-Anarya problem, and still others publish articles and texts and try to take the issue back to a few hundred years. All of them do not know the social aspect of the Buddhism, the historical truth that Siddhartha, who opposed the extreme ritualism and varna system of the Upanishad period, became the Buddha to oppose these rituals. For the first time in the world, the idea that everyone is equal by birth, instead of relying on the karma of the Aryans, Buddha has practiced it by bringing the lowly like Upali,, Chunda, Chincha, Visiddhi Angulimala, Alavi, and Sujati in to Buiddhist Sangha/ community was a big revolution. Prof. Laxminarasu spoke about socialism in the Buddhist practices. Lakshminarasu noted that even language was not systematically developed at the time of Buddha to express many feelings. He has used terms like concept of Dependent Origination as 'PratityaSamutpada'. Brahmins spoke of past karma, rebirth, sins etc. But Buddha developed ideas like Anitya, Anatma and Nirvana to negate the Brahminical bigotry of Karma etc. Ramulu mentioned some of these in this book.

Marx and Ambedkar were intellectuals who came one after the other in the evolution of human civilized society. Few people have fully understood Marx in India and applied it to the diverse society in the country. Others like Kosambi also postulated that the Brahmins peacefully taught the natives agriculture and brought about change, while the Dalits and adivasis had refused food production and agriculture, therefore remained backward. This was criticized by many scholars like Deviprasad Chattopadhyay and some German scholars. A few Marxist scholars who have examined India under the Marxist mode of production have used relations of production to describe phases of historical develop-ment. But, they have not been able to say which social class or caste is involved in production process and the value of the goods manufactured by them in relation to their social background. Even today Fishermen fish, blacksmiths, potters etc. had castes, occupations, products with caste labels. Dalits or untouchables on the other hand are not allowed to produce commodities or enter service sector on their own and were prohibited or blocked to enter market through religious rituals and practice. It is strange none of the experts have explained why the power is always enjoyed by those Trivarnikas from the very beginning till today. I don't know whether some Marxists wanted to say it or couldn't say it, but Marx in his first volume of Capital talked about India's caste-based production system, unlike the division of labour of Adam Smith where the process is divided in to 18 parts to produce a finished commodity. In India each caste has an occupation and the whole family produces the commodities and it remains static without any change. Marx clearly indicated the caste system that involved through caste-based occupations made the productivity unchangeable. He has given the example of a snail that wrapped its body in itself; likewise, the economic surplus had not been converted into capital to bring change. It was never discussed by top Indian Marxists. Perhaps because all the Marxist intellectuals of that time came from the same social class, did not understand the relations of production of the lower castes, but they preached Marxism like a Veda. Some of them have failed to identify who are the exploiting castes and who are the exploited castes. May be some of them have unconsciously handed the nation to the fundamentalists without much ideological struggle. Babasaheb Ambedkar is perhaps one of the oldest scholars who studied Marxism in 1913-16 in Columbia University in America. He studied the subject Marx, Post-Marxian Socialism in M.A. The Russian October Revolution did not happen at that time. The intellectual class in India (who are called like that by birth) who read books brought by someone, many absurdly translated the works of Marx from German to English and incompletely translated into Telugu etc. Unable to develop a class analysis, they struck at a level. In fact, Ambedkar tried to apply Marxism to India, imbibing the ideas of the Labor Party, built with Fabian socialists who practiced Marxism during his university days in England. As Acharya Murjaban Jal has said in an article in EPW that Ambedkar was the Indian Gramsci and the Brahmin over lordship of Left parties ignored him. Now the work and Agenda of Ambedkar, Phuley has to be carried by the large number of Dalit – Bahujans, the social proletariat and intellectuals who are being subjected to socio-economic exploitation need to struggle hard both in intellectual field and in practice. This is a book that teaches this particular historical duty for today's youth, activists and Dalit Bahujan intellectuals. Sri B.S. Ramulu has done a good job in writing this book. I congratulate him.

Innovated in India
Social Philosopher

- Dr. Katti Padma Rao

Marxists have diligently neglected the socialism of Buddha. Ambedkar declared that Buddha was a great socialist. Ambedkar discovered Dialectics in Buddha. Ambedkar formulated the science of Socialism in Buddha.

B.S. Ramulu has applied Ambedkar's thought to the modern society and explained it in detail in this book. BS Ramulu thinks in a new way. He was an activist who studied Marx, Engels, Lenin and Mao. A modern social philosopher who studied Buddha, Mahatma Poole, Ambedkar, Periyar Ramaswami Nayakar and Narayana Guru.

His is analytical style. His analytical method is descriptive. There are formulations in this philosophy. His life experiences, hardships, studies and understanding are reflected in his writings. B.S. Ramulu saw society deeply. Hegel discovers the contradictions in society from kinetic theory. He concluded that caste antagonisms were stronger than class differences in society. He concluded that the Communists could not bring about socialism without a caste-eradication way of life. If socialism comes, not only economic problems will disappear, but all social, economic, cultural and philosophical differences should be eliminated. "It is not possible for Indian communists to study Buddhism", Ambedkar

said. Sri B.S.Ramulu is a constant student. A prolific writer. His is a synthesis method. Synthetic method of speech can combine many concepts. He has a sense of logic. Marx and Engels also did the same thing in their time. Dr. B.R. Ambedkar also did the same in his time. That is why there is an integrity in their writings. This synthesis, coordination and integration has been continuing since the beginning of Buddhism. In his work, we can see not only Hegel's kinetic theory but also Kant's theory of knowledge. He is an honest and sincere writer. It will be in his writing. He included the analysis method of German Ideology by Karl Marx. He is bold in applying the philosophy to the society. He applies Buddha's Pitakas like Panchasila, Ashtanga Sutras, Long Dialogues, Jataka stories, Vinaya etc. to the modern society. A new innovation is the way Buddha is described as a great socialist. Ambedkar wrote the essence of Buddha and Dhamma. He took hold of the educational wisdom of Mahatma Phule. His study has arguments and counterarguments. He was an anti-humanist theorist. He concluded that there is no order of production in the way of life of Trivarnas. It is said that sociology is born out of the living cultures of the forces of production. This book suggests a new way to the readers.

B.S. Ramulu has a big heart, Innovative trajectory,A critical perspective, and a Vidhwat language. Linguistics. That is why his works awaken the mind. BS Ramulu encourages writers widely and Wrote hundreds of prefaces to many books.–After Dr.C. Narayana Reddy, he published more books in Telangana. B. S. Ramulugaru. Ditta with correspondence,He has an amazing memory. He lives like a university.

He speaks like a preacher from the time he gets up in the morning until the night falls.He Keeps writing, which keep analyzing. Sometimes they go in favor of the society and sometimes they go against the society. B.S. Ramulu is also very introspective. Women are respected. My friend Swarna Kumari is treated as his younger sister. Shushrusha quality is also there. When I underwent a knee operation at Hyderabad Apollo Hospital, they used to come and sit and cheer me up every day. In the seven years we were in Hyderabad, there was not a day when we did not talk. At least we have co-ordinated a hundred times. His wife Syamala is also like my own younger sister. Ours is a family friendship. He was on every platform when the Andhra Pradesh Dalit Women's Association was in full swing from 2003 to 2007. That movement is the reason why house plots, pensions and all welfare schemes are given in the name of women in Andhra Pradesh today. Andhra Pradesh Dalit Women's

Association in Hyderabad N.T.R. When a Mahasabha was held in the grounds with 50,000 people, he presided over that assembly. He was the principal when socio-political classes were held for 15 days in Ponnur. He also acted as the principal when the Andhra Pradesh Women's Association conducted classes at Lumbini Vanam in Ponnur. B.S. Ramulu was a modest creature. He is a great friendly character. His conversations are lively. There is a strong association with Guda Anjaiah, Gaddar, Wangapandu Prasad and Masterji. They also worked together during the Telangana struggle. It is his continuous activity to coordinate and integrate Telangana poets and writers. Many research papers have been published on his books. B.S.Ramulu in all academic disciplines. Ramulu's social, economic and cultural contributions are being worked on. He is a good storyteller. A sentimentalist. Rahul Sankrityayan novel narrative is in him. He is a psychoanalyst. Kahlil Gibran and Kabir appear in his works. At times, psychology overshadows his writings. He also worked on social personality formation. Wrote many books. That is why he was able to say Buddha's socialism. Karl Marx "Investment has philosophical functions. Engels's "Dialectics of Nature" contains the contradictions of natural life. Understanding these and applying them to the Indian society started only after the 1985 Karachendu movement. Those who have taken more steps in that direction are B.S. Ramulu Garu.

B.S. Ramulu studied Buddhist philosophers like Dignada, Vasubandhu, Nagarjuna, Dharmakirti etc. His is an extensive philosophical study. He observes many changes coming in the society from time to time and interprets them in his writing. He performs his duties as a kinetic historical physicist. That is why his writings are up to date. Steyr Baktsky of the Soviet Union compiled, compiled and edited Eastern philosophies and provided readers with a comparative analysis of the comparisons between Western and Eastern philosophies. Among such volumes, the two volumes "Buddhist Logic" are very important volumes. How "Buddhist Logic" has reached the highest peaks has been presented in a comparative study with Western philosophy and logic sciences. Because BS Ramulu incorporated the details of those volumes in his analysis, they are at a level that no one else can reach. Philosophical and logical analysis continues.Mao wrote on Kinetic Physicalism called Contradictions.Stalin wrote about Dialectics. Lenin elaborated on Dialectics on many occasions. All those works were influenced by BS Ramulu Dialectical Philosophy. Carl Ford, a Russian writer, wrote a great book on materialism. That the effect of the text is also B.S. Garu is on.

B. S. Ambedkar's writings on caste eradication, caste problem in India, who are the Shudras, who are the untouchables, the knots in Hinduism, Buddha and Dhamma, What Congress and Gandhi have done to the untouchables are well read. He was influenced by Plato. Many concepts of Plato's ideal kingdom are updated in his writings. If written like Gudipati Venkata Chalam's musings, thousands of pages of philosophy will be told. He was exposed to the concept of avoiding the suffering of people in Buddhism. He was influenced by Mahatma Phule Gulangiri. He opposed caste and Brahmin rule in his writings. Many plans were written on movement structures. His style of writing does not include quotations (footnotes). He digests the writers and speaks in his own language. Noting that caste is a hindrance to the construction of socialism, he strongly asserted that there was caste rule in the Naxalite movement. After the Karachedu movement, KG Sathyamurthy, BS Ramulu, U. Sambasivarao, Kanche Ilaiya, who were influenced by the communist movement, fought against caste. .S.Ramulu ran a magazine.His stories depict life. His. mother was a beedi worker.His father died when he was young. His paternal uncle,was a supporter of Achala.His influence was on BS Ramulu.There is pain and truth in Achala too. BS Ramulu's writings on Marxism now have lessons for communists.

"Communists are not abandoning their caste. Communists are not abandoning religious concepts. Communists are not losing their obsession with property. Most communists are not following Marx's theory," he charged. That is true. Change will come through the works of B.S.

Let's hope. B.S. Ramulu became the chairman of the Telangana BC Commission and after independence, BC commission reports were published in Telugu. The economic, political and social injustices that are happening to BC are being raised now. He wrote 'BC Notebook' and his opinions are honest. B.S. Ramulu Kandukuri Veereshalingam and Gurjada Apparao are constant writers. He always recites philosophy like Potuluri Veera Brahma. Future productions will also be in his writing. The influence of the communist plan was on him. He studied Karl Marx's Capital and Capital both economically and socially. He also studied Greek philosophy. The thoughts of Socrates, Plato and Aristotle are reflected in his writings. His is the method of synthesis. The sub-narrative trend of Ramayana, Bharata and Bhagavata is also seen in his works. That is why there is extension in his writings. His works are Philosophical Doctrines. His writing style is well researched. Like Dasarathi Rangacharya, is capable of making philosophy narrative. Like Kaloji, Telangana is known for its reputation. He likes Telangana. He wrote a lot on Telangana language, history, culture and politics. They are compasses for generations to come. That is why B.S. Ramulu is called a 'University of Social Philosophy '. I like him very much. Because there are few people who write continuously in depressed races. There are few people who write or print. Those who publish are very few. B. S. did these two tasks effectively.

Dr.G.R.Krishna Gogineni
Professor of Eminence & Founder Director,
A.J.I.M, Mangalore
Research charge 'D' affairs.
I.D.E.S., Brussels, Europe

Original Contribution

I have read the book with intense interest on "Buddhism-Socialism and Ambedkarism" by B.S.Ramulu. The book is a collection of some research papers, written on different occasions and now edited into the book and published. However, the book attained the status of a unique thesis on "Buddhism - Socialism" etc., with great cohesion and flow of argument on the subject The thesis shows decades of extensive reading on the subject by B.S. Ramulu. It also reveals his authority and the clarity on the subject, which is rare in the philosophical writings of modern Telengana and Andra.

In the chapter on "Buddhism -Socialism" the philosopher Ramulu comprehensively analysis the evolution of human thought, both in the west starting from Greek and in the east starting from Buddha. The paper traces Boudham and it's flourishing through 17 centuries in human history. Ofcourse the paper ends with Ambedkar study and his inspiration from Buddhism.

The other comprehensive paper on "Ambedkarism and Socialism" traces the inspirations and social influences of Ambedkar behind his turning into Socialism and Buddhism including the assessment of B.R.Ambedkar as an eminent economist and philosopher.

The whole subject starting from Buddhism to Socialism to Ambedkarism is discussed and analysed, in the light of classical Buddhist doctrine of "Prathitya Samutpada". This is a marvelous original contribution to socialism and Ambedkarism. The paper ends with the analysis of modern Indian society and latest Telengana society after the Telengana successful movement.

In short, the book is a very original contribution by the social philosopher Ramulu.

I whole - heartedly commend the book for all interested intellectuals on the subject not only in India but also in the Europe, the USA and all the rest of the english speaking world, as the book is translated into english also on the same title.

15th July 2023   **Dr.G.R. Krishna Gogineni**
'Shanthi Siddhartha' Hathill   Cell: 91 7259 184 672
Mangalore -6

An important contribution in the process of developing basic theory.

- Dr. Bharat Patankar.

Social philosopher B.S. Ramulu's book is a part of the all India trend which is gradually developing during last 50 years in India. It started late 1960s and early 70s with Prof. Gail Omvedt writing on caste system in India in 1966 and continued with "Cultural revolt in Western India..." Calling caste system as a mode of production in 1972-73.

This was followed by com. Sharad Patil writing about 'Marx, Phule, Ambedkarism' in late 1970s and early 80s. He continued to develop his theory further and reached the concept of the 'Sautrantric Marxism 'during early 2000s. In tradition of all these developments B.S. Ramulu has written this book.

"**Buddhism, Socialism, Marxism, Ambedkarism and Pratitya Samutpad**" A perspective needs to be developed today.

He is dealing with the theoretical developments in the methodology of analyzing society wright from Buddha and continuing up to Babasaheb Ambedkar. This is an admirable attempt and an important contribution in the process of developing basic theory.

I thank him for asking me to write about the book.

Buddhism
Socialism
Marxism
Ambedkarism

Buddhism Socialism

What is Socialism?

Socialism is a political philosophy and movement encompassing a range of economic and social systems. Buddha (563-480 BC) prophesied that one should take refuge in Budham, (wisdom), Dharamam (reality that we live) and Sangham (Community). Babasaheb Dr. B.R. Ambedkar said that he drew the principles of freedom, equality and fraternity, which define democracy and socialism, not from the French Revolution, but from Buddha. Abraham Lincoln extended the definition of democracy as 'for the people, of the people, by the people' and said that social justice, social change, and peaceful transformation that provide the fruits of development and knowledge to all should be the fundamental goal of democracy. By Ambedkar's definition, the aim of democracy was transformed into socialism. It can be defined as Buddhist Socialism.

Buddhist socialism is still practicable today. Memorable and acceptable. Not stopping with Sangam Saranam Gachchami, Buddha emphasized social justice, social life, and its significance by saying

Buddhism Socialism

'Dharmam Saranam Gachchami'. Buddha gave the highest importance to wisdom and knowledge by saying Budham sharanam gachchami. That is why the era of Science continued during the flourishing period of Buddhism. Even today, Buddhism continues to be the era of science. It may be noted that Dr B. R. Ambedkar's birth day was declared as **World Science Day** by the United Nations.

Buddhism accorded importance to education, science, medicine, social harmony, life values and culture. Those people inspired, established Buddhist universities and viharas. Thousands of people studied in these universities for centuries. Famous scientists worked as professors in Buddhist universities. Buddhist universities had many branches. They were called gates.

The well-known historian Mallampalli Somasekhara sharma (1891-1963) has given many details in his discourse essay 'Buddhist Universities in Ancient India'. Komarraju Venkata Lakshmana Rao (1877-1923) wrote books classifying history into three eras namely Hindu era, Muslim era and British era before the Indus civilization was discovered in the excavations of that time. There is a religious perspective in writing Hindu age. It may be noted that British era cannot be written as Christian era. It is not correct to use the word 'Hindu' in history and literature referring to the period before tenth century. Al Beroni (11-) was the first to use the term Hindu in his writings. The word Hindu was derived from the word Sindhu in Arabic. The word Sapta became Hapta. Thus, the words Sindhu and Hindu started as a word related to the Indus River and the Indus region. The word Hindu does not appear anywhere in written literature and history till the 10th century. Modern Indian History Scriptology (Histeriography) has been taking its shape from 1850-1870 AD. Since then, history is being written by separating as Hindu kings, Muslim kings and Britishers with the religious prospective expressing love for some and hatred for others. It is important to note that adding the word 'Hindu' to the ertswhile history prior to 10th century with the religious perspective is to promote the Hinduism and supremacy of the Hindu Varna based system. Much of the history was not written in a Hindu tone before the 10th century. Writing history on the basis of Vajmayam words in Pali, Prakrit, Brahuvi, Dravidian and Sanskrit languages would bring it close to the history. Words in a language do not evolve that rapidly. So language evolution is trustworthy.

B.S Ramulu

Those who take evidence from Sanskrit for writing history, unknowingly get stuck in Hindu religious propaganda and ideology. It is not easy to get out of such influence. Therefore, the development of history is closer to the facts in writing based on scripts of Brahuvi, Pali, Prakrit, Dravidian languages, Brahmi, Kharosthi, Khmer, Burmese, Thai, Sinhala, Latin languages and scripts.

The contribution of Rhys David (1843-1922) of England to the Pali language is exemplary. He was employed in Sri Lanka in 1863. Thus, be became interested in the Pali language. He became an expert in it. From 1892–1904 he worked as a professor of Pali language at London University. He extensively explored Pali language literature and Buddhist literature and wrote many works. Perhaps, Rhys David is a trailblazer introducing Pali and Budhism to Europian society. The Hindu religious perspective which started from the Indian independence struggle of 1857 spread in the national movement of the Congress and Historians such as K.P. Jaiswal in his writing promoted the self-respect of ancient Indian history as Mahojwala Hindu religious history. In fact, all of them are related to Buddhist, Varna, caste, and histories which are not related to the word 'Hindu'. Historical facts brought out by Rhys-David couple were set aside by Hindu Varna fundamentalists while giving importance to the supremacists for Hindutva propaganda. Ramayana and Mahabharata, which took a modern form long after the Buddha, have been ascribed antiquity by pushing them back a few thousand years and a few yugas.

Buddhism thought that knowledge should be useful to people. It was put into practice. People of many countries, many kingdoms and many religions studied in these universities with freedom, equality and self-respect. From there, knowledge spread throughout the world through them.

By that time, the matriarchal system was replaced by tribal societies. The male-dominated patriarchal system was set. Buddhist socialism, Buddhist dharma and Buddhist culture have enlightened the world for centuries as part of the patriarchal couple system. It can be said that Buddhism is the first socialist system built by human beings. The role of Universities (Vishwavidyalayalu) along with Buddhist monks in the spread of Buddhist Socialism was paramount.

Buddhism Socialism

Iron Age - Rural Fixed Farming:

Harappa, Indus Civilization BC. Created a great human civilization over a period of 3000 years. They did not know iron. They knew how to pump water through pipes and making of porcelain vessels by melting them at 1400-degree heat. Such a great civilization has collapsed. Then, after many centuries, minerals and metals were extracted and many new products were made. In 7th Century or in 10th century BC, iron was discovered. An iron stick and a plow were invented. As a result, fixed farming has increased in place of weed farming. Fixed farming promoted a rural self-sustaining economy. In the process of stabilization of the caste system, caste based professions as the foundation, the rural self-supporting caste economic system, the self-supporting rural socialist system, professional skills evolved over centuries, products and services were on the sublime raise. Till 1810 i.e. 60 years after the beginning of the industrial age, goods were being exported from India to other countries of the world. Although caste, class and color distinctions persisted in the rural self-supporting economy, it was a self-supporting socialist system even to those limitations. Even today, its remnants can be seen in the villages where everyone, regardless of caste, lines up and addresses each other as if they were blood relatives.

Socialism at Takshasila (Takkashila) University:

Community life and socialism continued in the 10th century BC in Takshasila (Takkashila) University. As early as the 5th century BC, King Taksha of Tashkent of Russia was influenced by the Buddha's teachings and established Taxila University. Chanakya as a teacher and Maurya Chandragupta as a student studied there. Where is Pataliputra! and Where is Taxila! It is needless to mention the fame of the university as they traveled hundreds of miles and studied there in those days when there was no transportation facility. Knowledge of various forms of sciences spread throughout the world through Taxila University. One of the main reasons why there is uniformity of many words in different ancient languages is because of the spread of the education learned at the University of Taxila. Charaka, famous for Ayurveda, also studied as a student and worked as an Acharya (Professor) at the university.

Socialism during the reign of Emperor Ashoka:

Emperor Ashoka (304-232 BC) converted to Buddhism after the Kalinga War and worked towards spreading Buddhism throughout the subcontinent. We read in our text books that Ashoka got the trees planted on both the sides of the road, got the wells dug and got the roads built. All these are development welfare programs taken up as part of Buddhist Socialism. He contributed to the autonomy of Taxila University.

Buddhism spread democratically into several foundations. Mahasabhas (Buddhist music) were held with the Buddhists from time to time codifying and harmonizing the Buddhist teachings, way of life and culture and continued to diverge into separate branches.

Socialism of Socrates, Plato, Aristotle:

Socrates (470-390 BC), Plato (427-347), Aristotle (384-322 BC) were great philosophers who grew out of Greece. Socrates is famous for saying that he knows that he knows nothing. He proposed an ideal society within the Greek kingdom. It was a period of continuing slavery. Plato proposed an ideal society not for slaves, but among slave owners. The Buddha did not abandon the slaves like that, but if they were freed with the permission of the master, he admitted them into the Buddhist community. Alexander's teacher, Aristotle, wrote many treatises. The modern world continues to depend largely on Aristotle's theories and understandings. Aristotle was a great philosopher.

Maurya, Satavahana and Pala dynasties who supported Buddhism:

Many royal dynasties like Mauryan dynasty, Pala dynasty, Satavahana dynasty followed Buddhism and encouraged. Whenever there were wars and conflicts on the raise, the importance of Bhakti Vira Rasa increased for peaceful transformation.

Nagarjuna Konda Sriparvata Vidyalaya:

After the fall of the Mauryan Empire in BC, the Salivahanas (225 BC – 225 AD), known as the Salivahana Empire, served extensively in the propagation of Buddhism under its influence. Schools were established at Nagarjunakonda and Sriparvatham. Over time it came to be known as Acharya Nagarjuna University.

Socialism by Nalanda University:

Buddhism Socialism

Nalanda University, which has been operating since 427 AD, had 2000 professors and ten thousand students in Rajagiri on the border of Bihar and Nepal. Founded by King Kumaragupta, Nalanda University gave major importance to socialist sciences. The Guptas and King Harsha of Kannaju nurtured this university. Nalanda University reached its peak during the reign of the Pala Dynasty kings in the 7th century. Many scientists were produced. Astronomy, medicine, science, metallurgy were extensively researched. They have led to many new skills and professions.

Vikramsila University:

Dharmapala (783-820) of the Pala dynasty founded Vikramsila University in the 8th century. Vikramsila Universityis a university known for its history. In 1193AD it was invaded by Muhammad Bakhtiyar Khilji. Knowing that the scholars here were more knowledgeable than their king, thousands of students and teachers were murdered by Bhaktiyar Khilji to ensure that no one should be more knowledgeable than their king. Heads were cut off. Around 90 lakh manuscripts, leather, copper, bronze and palm-leaf manuscripts were burnt. They continued to burn for three months. This is a great tragedy in history. The accumulation of knowledge was destroyed. Chinese pilgrims who worked as students and teachers and took away some texts to China were only left.

Buddhism respects women:

Buddha's mother is Gautami. When she questioned why women should not be included, women were also included in the Buddhist community. Walter Reuben in his book 'Slaves in India' written in Germany describes with some evidence about the slaves of India in BC. We know the slavery and exploitation that continues even today. Then, during that period, if the slaves were freed, they should be included in Buddhist monasteries and Buddhist communities, and it was revolutionary. All are equal after Buddhist initiation.

Buddha rejected the hierarchy of male-dominated varna and caste systems and practiced equality. From the Mangali caste, which is sometimes seen as a Shudra caste, Upali and Ananda were recognized as the main disciples. Badhasarpa-dashtas, hunters, robbers, thieves, and prostitutes were guided and included into Buddhist community. Thus Angulimalu and Amrapali became famous disciples of Buddha. The relic of Buddha was known from the borders of Nepal and Bihar to Khanapur in today's Adilabad district. Bavari left Sapta Godavari Island near Khanapur Godavari and returned to his native place after meeting Buddha.

The sciences and scientists who grew out of Buddhist universities:

Many scientists like Aryabhata, Kanadu, Kapila, Ashwa-ghosha, Dharmakirti, Dhignaga, Charaka studied in Buddhist universities and became professors and did research. The sciences, arts, theories and inventions proliferated under socialism are sublime. Students study in universities from the age of 10-15 years. Faculty and students in universities continued to have accommodation and meals. Thus, the socialist system has continued for centuries in educational institutions and temples. It taught the doctrine of dharma kartruva to the kings. Peaceful transformation, peaceful coexistence, benevolence, humane values are what Buddhism is all about. Not to steal, no to adultery and no to lie were the moral values were to the society by Buddhist socialism. When Buddhism is seen not as a religion, but as a Dhamma, a way of life, a culture of life, the Buddhist ascetics living in the Samsara life of the Buddhist monk communities, their personalities continue to live in peaceful coexistence with benevolence. For any state, any society, any system, peaceful coexistence, through social justice, social change is the ultimate aim, the ultimate goal.

The destination Socialist concepts before Buddha:

The roots of socialism before Buddha can be found in Charvaka and other visions and Upanishads. Many of the Upanishads brought forward atheistic rationalism. Sankhya, Nyaya Darshanas, Purvamimamsa, Uttara Mimamsa, Shad-darshanas, have atheistic, rationalist and socialist sentiments in their nature. From the time of the Indus Civilization to 300 years BC, socialist sentiments and socialist systems have continued with the early commune systems. These can be observed in the history being reconstructed through archaeological remains.

Life in Indus and Harappan Civilizations:

Thus, the socialist commune systems that emerged from the Indus Civilization, Harappa, Mohenjodaro Civilizations were damaged by fixed farming, fixed living, Vedic Aryan invasions, migrations and floods. Vedic Aryas emphasized nomadic pastoralism. They learnt farming later. Varna system was formed among them. All that order can be learned through the study of history. Trivarjis considered the local tribes, races, and Buddhists to be fourfold, Shudras and Atishudras. It is important to note that people did not think so of themselves.

Commune and Socialist Concepts in Historical Evolution:

Gana tribes, Janapadas, with the desire for a kingdom, were merged into the kingdom. The boundaries of the kingdom expanded. Kingdom and empire systems were formed. Buddha was born during the reign of the leaders of the Gana tribes and Janapadas. By the time of Buddha there were 16 Mahajanapadas. The two Maha Janapadas of Nizamabad, Bodhan and Assaka are also recorded in Buddhist literature. It was a time when tribes and great tribes were being merged and included in the state as part of federalism. The period of Nandarajas. That order expanded as Nanda dynasty and Maurya dynasty empires. Thus, the socialist commune sentiments that have continued in the course of history are widely available in Buddhist Jain teachings.

The world was greatly influenced by the Buddha's teachings. Christianity and Islam were born many centuries after Buddhism. Both of them have adapted a great deal from Buddhism. To be precise, Buddhism is like the mother of Christianity and Islam. Vedicism also borrowed a lot from Buddhism. Followed. 'Om Sahana Bhavatu / Sahanau Bhunatu / Sahaviryam Karavavahai / Tejasvi Navadhitamastu / Mavidvishavahai Om Shanti, Shantihi' we all chant together in Vedic. It is said that 'we will be together'.

Socialism, Social Justice Socialism:

If you look at the evolution of history like this... socialism, socialism is equality, social justice is socialism. Many people think that socialism is a theory born out of the industrial revolution. Either they all think of world history as centered around Europe or they are not immune to its influence.

Buddha, Marx, Engels:

Buddha's journeys and prophecies throughout his life for fifty years did not just go away. It has spread into many fields such as philosophy, logic, literature, arts, decorative arts, way of life, culture, personality development etc. Buddha's Animism is "Everything changes and there is evolution in interrelationship". The philosophical concepts of Pratitya Samutpada are clearly formulated.

B.S Ramulu

The role it played in Buddhist decorative arts, Indian literature and cultural arts is immense. Buddhism reached the highest peaks in the world in the logical sciences of Eastern countries. Nalanda, Takshasila, Sriparvata Nagarjuna, Vikramsila universities have given many sciences to the world! Students educated in universities have spread all over the world like sowing seeds. The role played by philosophy, logic and science in understanding the world is paramount.

The philosophies and logical sciences that have evolved in Buddhism every 500 years constantly being contemporary and maintained their superiority. Anatmavadam "everything changes", Pratitya Samutpada, are the highest formulations of logical sciences and philosophy. Pratitya Samutpada clarifies that an evolution takes place in the synthesis of many social and natural systems of motion. This principle has dominated the way we view the world for centuries and even today.

Starting with Ashwaghosha, Nagarjuna, Dighnagu, Dharmakirti, Vasubandhu, Telangu, Rice David couple, Professor Lakshminarasu, Dr. Babasaheb B.R. Ambedkar, Rahul Sankrityayan, Sharad Patil who founded the Satyashodaka Communist Party, Russian Star Batsky and many others strengthened, introduced and analyzed Buddhist philosophy and logic. From the Vedic Sanatana texts to Arvachina and so-called Hindu religious texts, classics can be mentioned as many as 220 texts in the ancient Indian subcontinent. These are... Vedas, Upanishads, Purvamimamsa, Uttara Mimamsa, Shut Darshanas, Samkhya, Nyaya Vaisheshika Darshanas. Ramayana, Mahabharata etc.

Millions of scriptures in Buddhism:

While millions of scriptures were burned and destroyed, more than 500 philosophical, logical, and decorative texts and classics of Buddhism were published in the world. Since the time of Emperor Ashoka, they were spread into the world.

Thus the Buddha's teachings, and the way of life of the Buddhists were codified in triptychs called Vinayapitaka, Suttapitaka and Dhammapitaka and the ways of life to be practiced by the human society. Ananda, Upali, Vasubandha, Acharya Nagarjuna and many others supported Buddhist philosophy and ways of life. Mallampally Somasekhara Sharma published a small book of discourses entitled

'Buddhist Universities in Ancient India' in 1953. It has recently been reprinted. The role played by Buddhist universities around the world, in the fields of education, medicine, knowledge, physics and chemistry is sublime. In 1956, on the occasion of the 2500th birth anniversary of the Buddha, the Government of India organized a well-organized seminar and the seminar papers were published as a book collection. In October of the same year, Ambedkar's Buddhist conversion festival was held.

Development of Vedic sciences with imitation of Buddhist sciences:

In Vedic, Varna, Kula and Manu Dharma Shastras, the educational system continued in Gurukulam style. Being a part of the Guru's family, carrying out Sushrusha and study any one of the sciences for ten to twelve years. It's like taking a tution and taking a private study. In Budhism, study in the universities exalted in a great social consciousness, organized energy, personal development. Thus, Buddhism has shaped man as a social being from the beginning.

Vedic and Varna dharma shastras have from the beginning given priority to the individual way of thinking and the individual way of life. In this way, from the beginning, Buddhism laid great emphasis on community, social personality development, and way of life. Many sciences have been created in collective effort. They gave light to this world. The influence of Buddhism on Greek philosophy was enormous. Buddhism is rich in dialogues of mutual benefit. The Greeks were a very small nation. The sound Hindu is a name given by outsiders. An Indian has never been called that. At present they are Varna Dharma. After that it was transformed into Kula Dharma, Karma Siddhanta, Reincarnation Siddhanta and Atmanism. They are called as Hindu.

Atheism and Rationalism in Indian Philosophies:

In Indian philosophies, many philosophies have proposed atheism and anonymity. No Idol worship in Sanatana Dharma and Vedic Dharma. Anatmavada continued to prevail like Atmavada in Atma and Anatma vadas. Sharad Patil has extensively studied the origins of the varna system and the term varna in his book 'Dasashudra Slaveri'.

B.S Ramulu

Science, Journey, Broadcasts Bringing Out New Things:

More than 150 episodes have come up in YouTube in Hindi in the name of Science, Journey and continue introduce many new elements and reconstruct history. On the other hand, R.S.S. Parivar formed an organization called 'Itihasa Sankalana Samiti' with hundreds of full-time intellectuals writing history, philosophy in favor of Varna supremacy, and writing about developments that came through Buddhism, without mentioning the name of Buddhism, and also combined thousands of elements of Buddhism into Varna Shastras, Varna and caste history claiming that as the achievement by Brahmins. Most of the authors of the Upanishads were not Brahmins. They do not even agree to call them Sudras. Even today Viswa Brahmins and Viswakarmas are strongly opposed to addressing themselves as Shudras. They argued that they were better than Brahmins in the Madras High Court for a long time. Therefore, just because Brahmins call others Shudras does not make them all Shudras. They are all creators. Community builders. In another way, it can be said that these Dashavataras are popular as part of Varna division and Vaishnava tradition. Basaveshwara said "Khayakam" is Kailasam. He said that all castes are one. The Bhakti movements of Shaivism rejected the Vedas, the Darshans and the Upanishads and also opposed. Many people hide this fact.

Indus, Harappa, Mohenjo-daro Civilizations:

While Borra Govardhan's youtube series "Science Journey" proves how great is the culture and science technology of the Indus civilization flourished two thousand years before the Buddha and before the Vedic and Vedic civilizations, they made all of them a part of Hindu religious propaganda and added comments suitable for them, mixed Buddhism, Jainism, Ajivakam, Atheism, Anatism, Kannadaism, etc and are claiming to be their own and promoting them. If you read the texts written by Chinese Buddhists such as Fahian Hiuen Tsang, Itsing, and later Alberuni etc., many Buddhist texts and English translations available in Tibet, Thailand, Japan and other countries, you will know that they are imitations of Buddhist scriptures called Hindu Dharma Shastras and Philosophy. So they are not made popular.

Therefore, the Buddhist countries have announced that they will give hundreds of crores of rupees as a grant to Nalanda, Takshasila,

Buddhism Socialism

Vikramsila and Acharya Nagarjuna universities to be renovated, modernized and also teach modern sciences.

Developments in Buddhist Culture:

Thus, Buddhist scriptures, Buddhist practice, Buddhist way of life, Buddhist culture have pushed the world forward in the age of knowledge and the age of science for centuries. Over time, thousands of books were burned when the Muslims invaded. Historians write that they burned for several months. As it was burnt to ashes, the texts that reached other places and other universities were only left behind.

Along with the Muslims, the powers that declared their superiority, many kings starting from the Gupta kings were oppressed under the influence of the Brahmins. From Buddhism to so called Hinduism a lot was incorporated. Except the Varna and caste systems, Manu Dharma Shastra, Atma, Reincarnation and Karma doctrines, all other things were changed from Buddhism to Hindu Dharma. Doctrine of dharmakartrutva as said by Maharaja Janaka in the Ramayana and in modern times by Gandhiji is drawn from Buddhism. It goes without saying that peace, non-violence, love and compassion belong to Buddhism.

Ramayana, Mahabharata, Puranas as reworked after Buddhism:

Linguists and historians believe that Ramayana, Mahabharata, Bhagavad Gita took its final form between the second and sixth centuries AD. It is explained with many details and evidence in the Buddhist 'Science Journey' that Vedas are not as old as they claim ie 1500 years BC, and the pronunciation of the letters in them were not born by then, Devanagari did not exist at that time, and they all belonged to the period after Buddha. They are shown from the original scriptures in Devanagari. Sanskrit scholars have concluded that most of the Bhagavad Gita was adopted from Buddhism and said by Malachi as a justification for the philosophy of Varna Adhikya. Dr. Malayashree understood that decades ago, published 'Manava Gita' in Sanskrit saying, 'Bhagavad Gita is not a human Gita'. Dr. Malayashree translated Ashwaghosu's 'Vajrasuchi'Upanishad into Telugu. T. Ravichand has done special work about Buddhism.

Ambedkar's conversion to Buddhism with 6 lakh people:

Ambedkar took 22 vows while accepting Buddhism. Dr. B.R. Ambedkar converted to Buddhism on 14 October 1956 on

Vijayadashami with six lakh people. He popularized Navayana Buddhism by writing the book 'Buddha and Dhamma' declaring that even if I am born a Hindu...I will not die a Hindu. Since then in India, spread of Buddhism, interest in Buddhism is increasing. Buddhism is now expanding as a strong doctrine and philosophy in India. Ambedkar made 22 standards for the adoption of Buddhism in accordance with the modern era so that even the common people could understand how the way of life should be and what kind of beliefs should be held from now on and six lakh people took a pledge. They are standards to liberate people from caste, caste, discrimination, oppression, inequalities and creeds that continue in the name of so called Hindu Dharma. Two decades ago in Nellore, Ingilala Ramachandra Rao Bodhi Ambedkar converted to Buddhism by thousands of people in the name of Buddhist Dharma Porata Samiti. Buddhist centers are emerging in Visakhapatnam, Kakinada, Mangalagiri, Nellore and other places.

Reconstructing Buddhism:

Buddhist centers flourish at Mahendra Hills in Secunderabad and Buddha Vana at Nagarjunasagar. Anjaneya Reddy, Annapareddy Buddhaghosedu, Dr. Kathi Padmarao, Kanche Ailaiah and others popularize Buddhist philosophy widely. All over the country and the world, they are getting rid of the dirty history and dirt and bringing forward the development of Buddhism in a bright light. Reprints of Ambedkar's writings started in 1991 on the occasion of Ambedkar's centenary and national and international conferences brought many novelties to the fore.

Socialism of Marx, Engels, Lenin, Mao collapsed within decades:

While Buddhist socialism continued for centuries in the Soviet Union, the socialist system established in 1918 under the leadership of Lenin and the socialist system established in 1949 under the leadership of Mao in People's China collapsed by 1985. Within a few decades they took a U turn.

Did they go forward with individual centric? Was it not based on socialist principles, culture and structure of social life like Buddhism, or was it because they depended on monarchy or its theory? Did the middle class intellectuals and educated people used the working class to come to power and become the leaders themselves? These are debatable points. Let's discuss them in the next chapter. Let us limit ourselves to the point that they collapsed within a few decades.

17 Centuries of Buddhist Socialism: While Buddhism lasted for 1700 years it continued to influence society till the 14th century AD. Some of the arguments that spread in the 11th century were the tyranny of Islamism and Muslim rule that caused irreparable damage to Buddhism and the country. Due to the Muslim attacks on Buddhism, the so-called Hindu Varna Dharma re-emerged, taking it as an opportunity. Bhakti movements started among the people in the country by synthesizing Buddhism, Islam, Greeks and Sufism against Muslim arguments. The devotional movements practiced by the people were different and the Bhakti movements practiced by castiest people were different. The bhakti movements of the Shudras were related to community-based socialism.

Bhakti movements taught us to see the divinity of man, humanity and humanitarian society, regardless of who were the kingdom. All these are adopted from Buddhism. Hindu varna-dominated devotional movements prioritized idolatry, the glory of the holy place and promoted it for the benefit of priests and merchants. Shudra Bhakti Movements 'One cannot be free from the sin of "Gochi" even if one visited Kashi' and denied the glory of the holy place and the glory of the rivers.

New definitions:
By today's definitions, the formation of Buddhist societies was one of the earliest prototypes of world socialism. Spartacus also proposed a socialist model of society. The model of socialism proposed by Buddhism continued for several centuries. Historians and anthropologists have confirmed that the "primitive communist society" proposed by Marxism never actually existed. Whereas European socialists and communists failed to know the existence of Buddhist socialist societies which actually existed.

A Socialist Manifesto with Philosophical Basis:
As mentioned earlier, it is the Buddhist society that had a global impact among the primitive socialist societies that were built by human beings with a socialist manifesto having a philosophical foundation. India had ancient connections with Greece, the birthplace

of European philosophies. By the time of the Buddha, Greek philosophy was at a rudimentary level and grew independently. Buddhism had a great influence on the Greek philosophers. Buddhism had taken strong roots as a strong social system here by the time of Plato and Aristotle.

In modern times, marxism related socialism as said by Marks, Engels, Lenin, Stalin and Mao was popularly known as Socialist system. The history of the preceding centuries was downplayed and shown. Now, in Russia and China too, the socialism that was then said has collapsed and democratic systems have been established. Now the power to spread out has lessened with the power of the state. Thus a new light is spreading on socialism of Buddhism.

Marx and Engels definition:
Marx and Engels were great human beings. They conducted many studies and brought forward many theories principles which could affect the word. With many studies, theories and formulations that affect the world have been put forward. They, pained by the hardship faced by the working class, for the sake of the welfare of the working class brought forward the contention of the working class. Since then, the workers of the world have gained many facilities during the Russian and Chinese revolutions. Reduction of working hours, improvement of workplaces, environment, security of life, holidays, provident fund, housing, free electricity, free canteens, profit share, bonus etc. were achieved.

Marx and Engels were at a young age with enthusiasm, and all the philosophers of the world until now interpreted the society in different ways. Marx said that the real thing is to change it. Marxists are very happy saying that. But the fact is that even Marx spent much of his life commenting on society but not towards changing it. Their knowledge is mainly indirect knowledge. Knowledge of books. There are few who believe the formulation of Marx to be true. Buddha worked towards changing the world. Christ, Muhammad, Guru Nanak and Kabir also worked to change the world. However, Marxists do not hesitate to distort history to any extent to maintain their ideological supremacy. It is evident form their stand to support Marx instead of condemning about the words said by him about the Philosophers. This is also evident that, in their fascination for Marxism, Marxists lose their own brain morphology knowledge and history.

Buddhism Socialism

Buddha was a practicing philosopher who recognized the need to change society. He observed the pitfalls of philosophical debates. He felt they were unnecessary. Budha was the first philosopher to Emphasize the supremacy of worldview over philosophies in the world. Two and a half thousand years later, Marx and Engels said the same thing.

Although Marx emphasized the worldview, Marxism relies more on scientific discussion than worldview. Buddhism emphasizes more on worldview. Marx said nothing more than what Buddha said. Ambedkar said this after a deep study of both. This point becomes clear even if you read only the third volume of Ambedkar's works. Few of the Upanishads discuss it in depth like that of the Buddha. But they did neither suggest nor commit themselves to social practice like Buddha.

Marx said nothing more than the Buddha:

Ambedkar analyzed and showed that Marx had nothing more to say than Buddha. There is sorrow in life. Ambedkar concluded by comparing Marx and Buddha that there is a cure for sorrow. If Marxism wanted a one-party dictatorship, it was Buddha and Ambedkar who worked to achieve democratic socialism in a multi-party system. That is why discussions and Mahasabhas were being held from time to time in Buddhism since the time of Buddha. Ambedkar called Buddha a great socialist builder. Ambedkar compared Marx to Buddha and made some formulations. Thus, it is implicitly said that Marx is equal to Buddha. Of course, Marx cannot be equal to Buddha. When compared with Buddha's socialist practice, Marx and Engels joins the ranks of academic scholars.

Buddha was a wayfarer:

Buddha traveled continuously for years, practicing and teaching what he believed. As if sitting in front of the TV, he sat in front of books and watched the world. Buddha left the kingdom, wife and children and devoted himself to social life. Marx lived as a part of the family, with his wife and children. Engels survived by running his own textile mills.

Because Buddha lived among people, he emphasized the superiority of love while providing medicine, education, friendship, and brotherhood. Marx and Engels could not live together with the people like Buddha. Therefore, they did not understand the ultimate meaning of benevolence, of being together with friendship, love, brotherhood.

As Jews, they could not be de-classed from their sense of superiority. So instead of bringing everyone closer like Buddha, they started criticizing and alienating everyone. If they had been among the people like Buddha, they would have included everyone like Buddha. Many new theories, propositions, philosophical concepts and philosophers have been discredited because of this failure and humiliated. Marx, Engels, Lenin, Stalin and Mao were not able to say or empasize about benevolence and compassion. Buddha, Kabir, Guru Nanak, Phule, Ambedkar, Lohia did this.

If Marx and Engels had worked like Buddha, a lot would have changed: the change in social life, like Buddha, if Engels had interwoven with the people, the egocrisis, the desire to prove that I am right, and the inhuman expression in their works would have reduced to a great extent. They loved their feelings. Those who opposed their sentiments were severely persecuted. Buddha loved people instead. He was able to transform thieves like Anguli Maludu etc. and was able to convert Amrapali and even the kings in favor of the people.

Buddha was not as narrow minded as Marx, Engels, Lenin and Mao. He asked not to believe what he said or what anyone else said. Gnostic Buddha said to believe and practice what is true. But Marx and Engels worked all their life to ensure that whatever they said was right. Buddha recognized the discernment and wisdom of society. But the notion that we are the only ones with the knowledge to think scientifically, egoism is widespread in the writings of Marxism. There is such a difference between Buddhism and Marxism in the theory of knowledge and belief in people. Marxism has no faith in the wisdom of people. Both Brahmanism and Marxism say that they are better than everyone else. That is why the Brahmins immediately adapted to Marxism. Thus, Marxism began to continue in the form of Brahminism in this country.

Buddha's Basic Philosophy:

As mentioned earlier, animism changes everything. Pratitya Samutpata Paropakaram Prema, Karuna, Panchsheela Ashtanga path are philosophical practices.

Buddha proposed a socialism that practiced Samata - Prajna - Compassion, Liberty Equality and Fraternity. Varna and caste systems are against them. They propose a society of differences. A four-color system was constructed for colorimetric purposes. As mentioned earlier, there was no word Brahmanism at that time. We are using this word for our convenience. The terms Brahmanism and Hinduism are recent. They are four color systems. Buddhists are showing evidence in recent TV episodes in the name of Science Journey that Vedicism, which came after the Harappa and Indus civilizations, is also of recent times and not as ancient as that. Buddhism proposed a middle way to achieve harmony between the lower classes and the upper classes. Marxism is a centralism which aims to achieve harmony with peasants, women, oppressed races,

regions, etc., who are marginalized rather than the working class.

Ambedkarism, feminism, Dalitism, classism, Buddhism and Marxism are not centrists. These are the arguments of the lower classes, and the arguments of the lower classes are called rethilibizilijidi shinililijiliri. Efforts are being made to transform Buddhism into centrist Marxism through grassroots classism.

Growth in Europe:

Buddhism has grown to incorporate the sciences from time to time in each century and did not collapse. Nagarjuna of the second century of the Satavahanas propounded Nihilism, Madhyamikaism, and many other philosophical concepts and analyzed. It took 1400 years for European philosophers to reach the level of Nagarjuna.

Kant-Hegel moved forward by reaching the level of Nagarjuna. Nothing that Hegel said is more than what Nagarjuna said. Nagarjuna advocated both Nihilism and Madhyamika at the same time. Hegel spoke of both nihilism and rationalism. Marx adopted nihilism and abandoned subservience. We will see this in detail in another chapter.

Europe developed late compared to India, Egypt, Greece and China. So socialist sentiments began to sprout in Europe a thousand years later. From the 14th century, Europe picked up speed from India, Greece and China. Europeans amassed the wealth of the world through robbery, rapine and trade in the Asian and African countries.

Modern socialist sentiments as part of European hegemony:

"Marxism is not the only theory that continued to seek European domination over the people of color. All the theories that came out under European domination in the last three centuries did the same. If we look at the theories of capitalism and liberalism, there is no need for separate evidence that their life journey is connected with the oppression and exploitation of Asia and other countries. Any kind of evidence is not needed. It seems that all theories have survived within the boundaries of power. Except those that were not born within these boundaries, all others are limited to those boundaries. Be it Adam Smith, Marxism, the theories of Rousseau, Locke, Hegel, etc., all have dealt with the spirit and ambitions of Europe. "It spoke of man, not of Europeans. Marxism created a system of wealth, equality, and peace for all mankind," says Ramamanohar Lohia (from Lohia's Vision 1).

The first communists were the slave-owning philosophers Socrates and Plato. It should be taken as the ignorance of Europe that Buddha, who was born two hundred years earlier and proposed and practiced the forms of socialism, was not discussed in the history of socialism. . Buddhism has guided the world in social, cultural, moral, economic and political fields.

Buddhism Socialism

Kingdom Incarnation Theories:

Buddha, much earlier to Socrates, Plato, and Aristotle, formulated the theory of state existence and development. Kancha Ilaiyya Ph.D. said that before Hobbes, Locke and Rousseau, he proposed the theory of the emergence of the social contract state, the theory of women's rights against Brahminism with the help of Anand, and the construction of the Buddhist society before Marx, the theory of the construction of a society of equal rights with socialist features. The thesis 'God as a Political Philosopher' can be understood by anyone who read the book. Ilaiyya's thesis, written from a Dalit perspective, poses a challenge to political philosophy so far.

Greek Dialectics, Dialectics of the Buddha:

Dialectics is the first meaning of dialogues. Socrates, Nagarjuna and others had philosophical discussions in the form of dialogues. Philosophical discussions from Buddha to Mahatma Jyotiba Phule and Jiddu Krishnamurthy used to take the form of dialogues. Over time the term dialectics became established. It is translated in Telugu as Gatitarkam instead of Gatitatvam (movement) as mentioned earlier.

Gatitarka in Greek is partly inspired by Buddha's Gatitarka. Buddha was the first philosopher, social scientist, political scientist and revolutionarywho widely discussed the fundamental kinetic principles of contradiction, evolution, quality and lack, applied them to life and practiced them as a worldly perspective. Socialism and dynamism taken from Buddha give us darshan in today's different socialist and marxist ideologies. We as Indians have to rewrite the history of world socialist society from Buddhism. The injustice done to Asian countries needs to be rectified. Materialism of the Charvakas, Marxists accepted materialism as well. Buddhism opposes materialism. Buddhism has made it possible to protest against materialism while seeking material development.

Uniqueness of Buddhism:

Buddhism practices socialism through love, wisdom, education, healing, and unity. Some socialists in Europe have proposed the same. Marxism, on the other hand, proposes socialism through enemy-hunting, hatred, imperialism, and confrontation. Psychology and subconsciousness as said by Freud, was a part of the worldview of philosophy in our country since the time of the Buddha. That is why our philosophies have simultaneously made man, mind, society and class fundamental.

Buddhism examines the individual, the class and the society in a holistic way and removes the need for the state from the society and the individual. Thus the way to the disappearance of the kingdom is easily possible through socialism for the Buddhist taluk. Christianity and Islam adopted the concepts of social practice through education, medicine and love from Buddhism.

Social equality movements in many forms:

Socialism and social equality movements continued in the form of religious movements and cultural movements in the world and in our country. Due to the absence of state power as a foundation, social movements lost their political form and took the form of religious, religious, moral and cultural movements. In how many years, how many generations, how many initiations, Ajanta and Ellora caves were created! Bambian sculptures and houses in Afghanistan are carved! We can only say it was possible only with a strong will and a stable life existed at that time with basic technology. We should imagine the kind of hard work and the passion to build Sarnath, Sanchi Stupam and Amaravati. If we could remember that in seventy years, we could not even build our own parliament building, it is needless to say how the buildings have been built over centuries attracting millions of people.

Many European countries have long been barbaric nations and races where tyranny and the use of force became their politics.

Buddhism, Christianity, and Islam born in Asia were responsible for the cultural revolution in Europe.

Even today social and political movements in our country are going on in the form of religion and caste. B. sp. A recent example is the movement starting from Ashoka till Basavadi, religions were spread for political purposes. Jyotibaphule's possession of Balichakravarti and Ambedkar's possession of Buddha indicate the pattern of social movements here.

Ambedkar's specialty:

Knowing the limitations of Europe and recognizing the importance of Asian countries, Ambedkar added Buddhist Dharma and Buddhist culture movements to his proposed socialism. We can also see the integration of Christianity and Islam into social movements and politics in recent struggles in South America, Afghanistan and Iran.

RSS and BJP raised hundreds of slogans like Ram Janmabhoomi. For the past 30 years, history books have been rewritten accordingly. The hatred fueled by Marxism took its toll as well.-Marxist socialism models depended on political domination, so it turned into a socialist culture that exploits people rather than through love, compassion, benevolence and service. A socialist culture should be the one that abolishes state power. It is not possible to build a socialist culture with Marxism based on state power. Buddhist Dharma, Buddhist Culture, Buddhist Socialism will correct the shortcomings of European Socialism.

Distinctiveness of Ambedkarism:

Ambedkarism is a modern form of socialism that has adopted the democracy of Buddhist socialism and the socio-economic arguments of Marxism in its own way. Ambedkarism serves as a worldview for building world socialism. Our discussion of Buddhism is part of

Ambedkarism. Thus Buddhism-Socialism also means socialism from Buddha to Ambedkar.

Marx's Imperialism:

Buddha was also a great statesman. There is one thing that Marx said in addition to Buddha. That is the argument of state power. Ambedkar rectified these errors and democratized the ideology of Rajyadhikar. Along with the democratization of statehood, Ambedkar emphasized the importance of Buddhism in social culture. Thus Ambedkarism became one of the most modern models of world socialism.

Marx believed in labor power.Aimed at kingship. Buddha believed in man. He believed in the humanity of man. From Angulimalu, he has lifted many from darkness, from hardened hearts to the human heart. Marx forgot the labor force of women. Thus Marx's theory of economic surplus value is incomplete and only with half truth. Scientists have made many scientific discoveries. Marx did not take their labor power and intellectual power under his purview. Thus the economics and philosophy of Marxism has become a reality. It has gone from a half- truth to a quarter-truth. By believing in the ideo-logy of state power, Marxism turned into authoritarianism.

It was also said that it was clearly a dictatorship in the name of the workers. The efforts made by the communists for the workers are tremendous. It should not be forgotten that many of the comforts and conveniences enjoyed by the workers and the middle class today are the result of the revolutions of Marx, Engels, Russia and China. In addition to these, Ambedkarism promoted the humanistic values of Buddhism and the democratic system. Ambedkar also made it very clear that state power is the key to unlocking all locks. But, it is not the dictatorship that Marx said. They are a democratic socialist system.

Buddhism Socialism

Buddhism is a socialist system:

Buddhism was a socialist system that promoted society by emphasizing an atheistic rationalist, anatma scientific way of thinking. It also includes level differences like Holtimers, People etc. The socialist system of Buddham Taluk is a patriarchal and male-dominated socialist system. Neither Marx's socialism nor Buddhist socialism in the sense of today's feminism is comprehensive socialism. Buddha was sympathetic towards women. It is necessary to recognize that Buddu, as a man of the day, had a historical limitation of masculinity.

Buddhism is not interested in state power, property or material comforts. Marxism relies on these three. Buddhism focuses on wisdom and benevolence. Therefore, instead of wanting to gain power, it has moved forward with a service perspective as the basic goal of providing knowledge to all, serving social culture and providing life. During the Buddhist period the requirements were less. By the time of Marx, Engels, due to less wealth and more industrial production, division of labor, class division increased. The needs have increased. Laws have increased. Hence, like Marx and Engels, Ambedkar also said that state power is the key to unlocking all locks.

Temple domes are for:

Vedics, priests and casteists created thousands of temples for their food and social supremacy to get honor more than the kings for generations. They got thousands of villages as donations from the kings and the authority to collect taxes from them. The wealth of thousands of villages was enjoyed by them for thousands of years. Bahujan Bhakti movements protested and opposed the looting of temples and shrines. Bhakti movements emphasized that God is not in temples and stones but in the heart of man and humanity.

Such upper castes say beautifully "Brahmin Bhojan Priya ". When they joined the Buddhist communities and the Buddhists became so, there was no difference between the Buddhist communities and the Brahmins. As a result, people lost special interest in Buddhism and became restricted to castes-based works and castes. Jainism and Buddhism lost their appeal. Such Buddhists and Jains were harshly suppressed by Muslims and Varnaists. Some socialist sentiments are seen in the Shaivite and Vaishnava devotional movements of Basaveshwara, Ramanuja etc.

After that in England in 1380 socialist feelings started to grow. Basavayya propagated Chapa Kudu's theory of social equality without distinction between castes to establish Veerashaivism to expand his political power. Kabir, Guru Ravidass, Guru Nanak, Potuluri Veerabraham and Vemana promoted social equality in the spirit of Sufis.

Hypothetical Socialists: (PRASAD)

After the Buddhist tantric and devotional movements in our country, the utopian writers in Europe in the 15th, 16th and 17th centuries expressed communist sentiments. Sir Thomas More (1478-1539) expressed socialist sentiments. Peter Chamberlain wrote a book called "Advocates for the Poor" (1649). He wanted to nationalize the king, property, churches, and declare forests and mineral wealth to be collective property for the poor people.

During the Saiva and Vaishnava Bhakti movements, socialist revolutions were carried out in the form of devotion by the lower castes in our country. Practicing socialism within the caste was natural. Bhakti movements protested the Buddhist Jains but worked to build socialism within the caste into socialism between castes. They advocated social equality of those who adopted their religion that they were all equal regardless of caste. As the revolutionary and romanticism of the devotional movements weakened, the socialism achieved among the castes shrunk into a socialism limited to the caste.

Thus, the Saiva Vaishnava societies split and split and contributed to the increase in the number of castes.

Socialism limited to caste:

One may be doubtful whether there will be socialism limited to caste. There is also socialism limited to the family. A mother can see all her children equally. If someone else comes hungry, she would not fast and serve him the food. Members of an organization, members of a class, members of a party, members of a caste can practice socialism limited to themselves. The fact that he is not a member of our party and that he can be considered as anything else indicates that his party has a limited socialist practice. If all brothers in the family on property have equal rights, then is a practice of socialism limited to the family. It will be true family socialism if their sisters also have equal rights in it. Without it, socialism is confined to the men of the family.

Male dominated devotional movements:

Bhakti movements were subject to the constraints of maintaining male hegemony. That was the time limit of that day. Bhakti movements helped male gods take the place of female deities. Women who invented agriculture like Pochamma, Ellamma, Kattamaisamma are being worshipped without knowing the names of their husbands. Their popularity was damaged by Bhakti movements. They were looked down upon.

Bhakti movements reduced the importance of women. The sexual process was performed by the gods. While one is glorified as the husband of 16 thousand gopikas, it is said that the penis of the other has played with all the heavens. He who amused thousands of women was worshiped. Likewise, Rambha, Urvashi, Menaka and Tilottham, who entertain lakhs of people all the time, should be worshiped many times. But Bhakti movements could not do this.

B.S Ramulu

Bhakti movements transformed women's language into a male-dominated one. The expression that shifted from songs to poems became male-dominated. The poetic structure of expression is against the language of the oppressed castes, the language of women. When the upper castes came to the leadership of Bhakti movements, their progressiveness came to a standstill. Nannaya came forward as part of the suppression of Indian, Buddhist and Jain feminism.

Muhammadan invasions:

Muhammadan invasions are associated with Bhakti movements. Equality among Mohammedans is socialism, Sufism attracted the people. A sort of social equality continued with backward consciousness in the tribal tribes as well. On the other hand, the egalitarianism built by Buddhism was still lingering. All these had an impact on Bhakti movements. Bhakti movements also opposed Muslim fundamentalism. That's how the Sufi way was born.

While Islam and Christianity came to our country, Buddhism came in new forms. But both of these are different from the Buddhist theory of knowledge. Guru Nanak's Sikhism, Akbar's Sufi path and Bhakti movements were formed with the propositions of social equality. Social equality in Islam and Sikhism attracted people. Socially degraded castes, ex-Buddhists, untouchables, and wild tribes who were socially degraded in the caste system joined Sikhism, Islam, and Christianity in millions. Although they were discriminated against in the first generation, they did not want to go back and return to the caste system as they gained social equality and brotherhood in their respective dharma after the second generation. Christianity is basically a branch of Buddhism.

The words integrity, integration and equality are words that are untouchable for the varna system. Therefore, apartheid could not keep the country united. There were two emperors who united India as a single country. One is Ashoka. Another is Akbar. Ashoka was a Shudra. Akbar was a Mohammedan. History is proof that if BC, SC, ST and minorities come together, the country will be united.

Buddhism Socialism

Shudras who ruled India:

In the book Bharatiya Charitra Shudra Drikpatham, it has been extensively explained that the makers of Indian history were Shudras, and that Indian kings and emperors were originally Shudras and Atishudras. Shudras and Atishudras only developed wealth, services, and skills. Brahmins, Kshatrhriyas and Vaishyas are the three varnas who never created wealth except they were wealth-eaters. In India, the kings and emperors appeared to be Kshatriyas due to their baptism by Brahmanism, but in reality, many of them were Shudras and tribals. Brahminism, based on the supremacy of ideology, dominated the society. They were in the positions of guiding the kings as royal gurus and ministers. In today's terms, they used to take over the central and state government secretariats and government departments. Ambedkar recognized the importance of Sudras and Ati-Sudras gaining a foothold in the bureaucratic government machinery.

Buddha was a tribal:

Buddha was a tribal, a folk. The period when Buddha lived was the period of the Janapadas. At that time, kingdoms and big kingdoms were not formed. If Kshatriyas, Vaishyas, Shudras and tribals brought together revolutions under the leadership of Buddhism for centuries, then the devotional movements, Islam, Christianity and Sikhism were revolutions brought under the leadership of Shudras. Especially today the castes belonging to the BC groups took the lead in all these.

Shudra Revolutions:

The Sudra revolutions in the form of devotional movements and adoption of paganism developed the languages of the respective ethnic groups in India many times over. First the Buddhist revolution and then the Sudra revolutions did immeasurable service to the development of Indian languages. Examining the development brought about by the Shudra revolutions in oral, folk and lyrical literature, it became necessary to bring Teluguness etc. in their poems.

Varnas who live by resorting to authority:

The Shudra revolutions, which were supposed to grow into the industrial revolution, remained incomplete. Jyotiba Phule, a Sudra, continued the course of history and sowed the seeds of the Avarna Revolution. With the leadership of Ambedkar, the Bahujan revolutions took a new turn in modern India. Ambedkar converted himself to Buddhism. Thus, the Buddhist socialism born under the leadership of tribals seems to have shifted to the leadership of Dalits.

In all three of the Kshatriya and Shudra Avarna revolutions in India, Brahmins played the role of revolutionaries as a group. When the results came in, they took the lead and profited. But it is true that Brahmins played a progressive role as some people.

Surviving by resorting to authority is the skillfulness of Brahminism. They resorted to the Shudra, tribal and Atishudra kings who came to power and elevated their caste. For example, Maurya, Ashoka, Satavahanas, Kakatiyas, Pallavas, Chaluk-yas, Vijayanagar kings, Reddy kings, Shivaji were all Shudras. Brahmins named them as Kshatriyas. As a result, casteization took place and ties between the castes where they were born and brought up were severed. It was easy for the Brahmins to win the king who was divided by caste with their words and deeds. This caused a lot of damage to the people. In the same way, the Shudras, who have recently become leaders, are being upcasted in the name of Marxism and are severing their religious ties with the castes they were born and brought up in. It became easy for the upper castes to win over the Shudra leaders who were separated by caste with their words and deeds.

Pushing the Shudras back...:

With the introduction of capitalism, the upper classes rushed to own the results of its development. So they started trying to reform themselves. English education and foreign contact contributed to this. Under capitalism, Shudras and Ati Shudras have lost in the competition of commodity production. With capitalism, the castes, who had been away from production for thousands of years, entered for new employment and ownership. As a result, Shudra and Atishudra castes suffered a lot. They are relegated to the lower levels of access and respectability. Foreign capitalism was a boon to the upper classes but a curse to the productive classes.

Even though Brahmanism penetrated the capitalist spheres of production, they could not elevate the social prestige of the Shudra and Atishudra castes, which were till then the sphere of production. The additional social respect that caste brought to the upper castes continued. Therefore, there is no need for the upper castes involved in the production to increase the social respect of the productive castes. It was the Shudras who undertook that work. Jyotiba Phule is a symbol of that.

Due to European investment, goods, commercial exploitation and wars, the Sudra revolutions led to loss of economic, social and wealth. As a result, the Shudra revolutions that were supposed to grow as capitalists, skilled workers and scientists were reduced to introverted devotional movements. They were reduced to scrambling for survival while fending off foreign invasions, looting and trade. The increased production and wealth of the Middle Ages were used by Hindu and Muslim kings and people for temples, domes, stone walls and wars. Even due to the destruction of Ganabajanas, fortress walls and festivals, the Shudra revolutions could not turn into new agricultural revolutions and capitalist revolutions. e.g. It would have been revolutionary if ponds and dams had been built instead of the Taj Mahal.

Industrial Age – European Supremacy:

Under European domination, modern industrialization took place in Europe. We have abundant human and natural resources. Had the

Shudra Atishudra revolutions here evolved into industrial revolutions, they would have been a guide to the world. Science and technology developed in a way that depended on human effort. The European industrial revolution was based on machines. Human resources have become unemployed. Moved manufactured goods to areas dependent on human resources. As a result, Shudras and Atishudras became unemployed here. Employers and workers benefited there. Thus, European capitalism is imperialist by birth.

The industrial revolution brought forth competition for the productive classes. The work done by man started to be done by machines. The name Shudras was given by others to the productive castes. However, Indians are called Hindus by others. 'Thus, some of the production castes and tribes were named Shudras. Many Shudras do not like to be called Shudras. Thus, they are forced to be called.

Shudras. Even today the Viswakarma castes, the representatives and symbols of the Mineral Age, oppose being called Shudras. As mentioned earlier, they led the case in Madras state that they were better than Brahmins.

Yuga division, Ramayana, Mahabharata:

The Yuga division of Krit Yuga, Treta Yuga, Dwapara Yuga and Kali Yuga is also related to Vaishnava tradition. It is not even 10-12 thousand years since humans started growing into civilized humans. But these yuga divisions, Ramayana, Mahabharata, history goes back a few hundred thousand years and wrote as if they all seem to exist. If they are written like that, it is clear that all of them belong to the post-modern metal age and mineral age writings. Weapons, jewelry, travel, agriculture etc. used in Ramayana, Mahabharata are all from AD. And existed by the sixth century. Not earlier than the B.C. sixth century. Hence Palini's Sanskrit grammar, which came out after Buddha, was written in the middle period of B.C. second century, and second century AD. All of the Sanskrit works which strictly follow Palini's Sanskrit grammar, date back to AD. After the second century. The poem Jayi with 8500 slokas was transformed into 24 thousand slokas in the 8th and 9th centuries as Mahabharata of lakhs of slokas. Production castes appear here and there in Ramayana and Mahabharata. The reason why caste discrimination appears in Ramayana and Mahabharata is that between the second century and the ninth century AD, the influence of Buddhism declined, and the influence of the Varna Vadis increased, adding up.

Period of Bhakti Movements:

The period of Bhakti movements and the period of Shudra revolutions are considered by some as the Dark Ages of the Middle Ages. Who made it the blind age? It is good to see who caused the light. The Dark Ages began with the entry of Europe into the lives of the Shudras. The productive castes were transformed into workers in the second stage. In the meantime, they were close to poverty. Industrial revolutions brought light to the upper castes who pushed Shudras into the dark ages. Hence, it was possible for the upper castes to take the lead in the social and economic spheres of modern India. Their 'caste supremacy' became another reason for their leadership in capitalist development.

Europe developed by robbing the world:

The industrial revolution of Europe started with the money looted from Asia, Africa, Red Indians and America. Especially since the 14th century, wealth as well as ideological, social, cultural and economic revolutions have shifted from Asia to Europe. Asia's eminence lagged behind. As the development in Europe was done with the wealth of Asia and other countries, the development of science there was done by taking the wealth of Shudras and Atishudras. European modern ideas are born from the riches of Sudra and Atishudra labor. But because of the superiority of Europe, the development of science was the superiority of Europe. Some of these details need to be checked.

B.S Ramulu

European supremacist socialist concepts:

Modern socialist sentiments in Europe, subject to European supremacy, began to blossom in the French Revolution of 1789. Vemana and Potuluri Veerabrahmangaru spread the ideas of socialism within the confines of the backward system, with backward caste limitations. In Europe, the movement created by Babouf, who was hanged in 1797, is called the neo-socialist movement by Europeans. Cabet Ykarian Communists tried to create an ideal communist society by building a colony with a population of 1500. It is like a Buddhist community. It survived for 47 years. Cabet said that the new society should be built by persuading the people by force of argument and by popular consent, not by tyranny. His sentiments are close to Buddhism.

The writings of British radicals (1756-1836) such as Goodwin Charles Hall (1756-1836) are a major development in the spread of European socialist sentiments. The concept of class struggle in its present sense was first expressed by Charles Hall, who wanted to nationalize the land. His explanations of the causes of war became a guide for later socialists. Poets like Wordsworth and Shelley also tried to spread socialism in their works like Vemana.

The next notable development in the spread of European socialism came in France under Napoleon. Saint Simon (1760-1825) suggested that the proletariat could be used as a tool for the establishment of a new society. In the case of property relations, he foresaw the theory that was developed by Marx and led the way for change. Charles Fourier (1772-1837) sought socialism and proposed phalancaries (self-supporting cooperatives) similar to the self-supporting rural society of our caste workers.

British Socialism:

Robert Owen (1771-1857) was the father of British socialism. He is also the father of the rationalist movement. Robert Owen wanted to achieve 'communism' by persuading the people. He also proposed a rural society like our Indian hamlets as a model of communism. He

Buddhism Socialism

said that a village should have 1500 acres of land. He bought 30,000 acres in Indiana, USA and established a colony called Nava Sammelanam (New Harmony) and made it a symbol of the communism he wanted.

The theory of European socialism also originated as social classism. It took a turn for economics. Formulations of European economists provided the basis for modern socialism. Socialism seems to be narrowed down from political and social science to economics. Sismandy (1773-1842) was hailed in the Communist Manifesto as the father of petty-bourgeois (small-scale) socialism. David Ricardo's economic writings contributed to the development of socialist economic theory. David Ricardo laid the theoretical foundations for the theories of surplus value and labor value. Based on these, socialists could deny that all profit is raw exploitation.

Hudskin (1783–1869), based on Ricardo's theories, made it clear that the worker is the sole creator of commodity value. William Thomson also said that he was an appraiser. John (1809-1895) was an American economist who adopted and further developed Karl Marx's formulation of commodity value in his theory of surplus value.

French economists Auguste Blanc (1805-1881) and Louis Blanc (1811-1882) proposed socialism with a slight difference. Blanky is the leader of the rebellion. He has no faith in elections. Louis Blanc advocated representative democracy based on universal suffrage. He wanted the revolution to come through the consent of the masses and winning through arguments.

Joseph Pierre Prodhon (1806-1865) played an important role in the spread of European socialist ideas. He was born in a poor farmer's family and educated himself. Proudhan was against the concept of 'government'. This fulfilled Marx's wish that the state should fall. Buddha said that the kingdoms would disappear, two and a half thousand years ago. Proudhan says that the politics is about domination, centralization of power and destruction of individual freedom. Socialist states also confirmed Proudhan's words. Communist and Naxalite politics also confirm Proudhan's prediction.

In this way, socialist theories such as Fabianism, Marxism, Guild Socialism, Feminism etc. were formed based on the theories developed by European intellectuals, leaders. Despite their faults, they were the mothers of European-style socialism.

Ambedkar Study Distinctiveness:

Even knowing all this, Ambedkar said that Marx said nothing more than Buddha. It means that Buddhist socialism brought such a great revolution. When it comes to Gati-tarkam, it took 1000 years in Europe to achieve the development in our country that was achieved during the period of Acharya.

Gatitarkam of Kant, Hegel, Marx was developed in our country during the times of Buddha and Nagarjuna. Capitalist economics could not develop in our country. Caste system, Brahminism, wasteful kings and people, foreign invasions and looting destroyed the economy here. Hence capitalist economics could not develop.

The field of Asian ideological ideologies was enriched by the likes of Mahatma Jyoti Rao Phule, Narayana Guru, Ambedkar, Mao, MN Roy and Ramamanohar Lohia. Europe, America and other countries are not ready to accept this word. If Ambedkarism, MN Roy, Lohia and feminism were combined in Indian Communism, India would have provided the ideological foundation and leadership for the subsequent world socialist movements. In Indian Communism this was hindered by the varnaism. However, this remains to be achieved. Buddhist socialism is very helpful as a historical basis for that.

Marx's Economist Socialism:

Some, such as Marx, have discussed sociology and state socialism as models of economics. But many in Europe discussed economics, the state, and models of socialism as a form of sociology. Recently, there has been criticism that the communists and Naxalites have indulged in economicism. In quiet, normal conditions, the revolutions that Marxism advocates shrink into economicism. The Russian and

Buddhism Socialism

Chinese revolutions were national revolutions. Their relation to Marxism is like the relation of Bhagavad Gita to our national movement. Many young people even got hanged in the fight for freedom of this country with the inspiration of Bhagavad Gita!

Marxism says that socialist revolutions will come only if Marxism is practiced. Buddha said, on the contrary, "know yourself, know this world, don't believe what someone says and only believe what you have proved to be true". There is a difference between Buddhist socialism and Marx's socialism. This difference is reflected in party structure principles, world view, social practice and system structure.

Let us recall once again:

Both Buddhist Socialism and Marxism Socialism are based on Gatitarkam (mobilism). Buddhism considers all inter-relationships with the vision of Pratyya Samutpada. Marxism and Engels, as supreme human beings, sought the construction of a new human society, but the clash of Marxism was fundamental in the conflict of unity. Buddhism says unity is fundamental. "I say relationship is fundamental in conflict". Buddha said that force should not be used as a foundation but wanted to bring about change through the consent of the masses. That is why in Buddhism the emphasis is on the intellect. In Marxism, confrontation is fundamental, and force is the decisive factor. Buddha wanted to win through love, by loving people. He wants to win even the enemy through love and truth. Marxism achieves unity among people by achieving unity in hating enemies. Thus, when the enemy is defeated, the foundation of unity disappears and the unity among the people breaks down.

Marxism wins people's hearts through sacrifice. Buddhism wins the hearts of people by imparting knowledge through sacrifice, service in medicine, education and other fields. Marxist socialism relies on state power. Buddhist socialism relies on human beings. Marxism says that the state should disappear while relying on the power of the state. Buddhist Socialism based on man is necessary for the disappearance of the state. Buddhist socialism is based on human being. Buddhist socialism thus constructs a worldview of life, society, and culture in such a way that the state disappears in life. Therefore, by merging Marxism, Socialism - Buddhist,Socialism a new society, social relations and culture will emerge where the state will disappear. Ambedkarism, which developed Buddhist socialism according to today's conditions, is related to world socialist construction. Ambedkarism is socialism achieved in a multiparty democratic system. These shades can be clearly observed in the Constitution of India. To make the Constitution of India a secular socialist constitution, the influence of socialist revolutions in Europe, Indian roots and developments in the history of Buddhism played a major role.

In the light shown by Buddha and Ambedkar, Marxism included feminism and Bahujanism and eradicated internal colonialism. A true advanced democracy would be socialism. This is what we mentioned in 1992 as a 'United Platform of Dalit Writers, Artists, Intellectuals' working against all caste, caste, gender, race, religion, region, country, language, discrimination and inequality.

(Published serially in Buddha Bhumi Monthly 2021-2022 issues)

Marxism – Socialism

Marx and Engels were great humanists. They studied world history in depth. Various sciences like philosophy, semantics, human values, human culture, civilization etc. were studied in depth. They studied the new ideas and inventions of their time, industrial revolution and capitalism from many angles. It was observed that the labor power of the workers is the source of wealth creation. It is concluded that wealth is created by human labor and in capitalist society workers are the creators of surplus wealth. Marx and Engels were shocked to see the suffering of the workers and the way they were being exploited.

They wrote extensively with pen and voice on behalf of the workers. Speeches were made. They hoped that a great socialist society would emerge under the leadership of the workers. They strongly believed that under the leadership of the working class, a system of proletariat dictatorship should and would be established. Capitalists, landlords, slave owners, and exploiters were outlawed. They proved that the producers of wealth for thousands of years are the workers. They studied the history again. Nature popularized evolutionary history as 'kinetic materialism'. As a way of re-examining the course of human history, the perspective became known as 'kinetic historical materialism'. After Marx, Engels's writings and the proposals they made, created a strong influence around the world. Labor groups have mobilized everywhere. Marx elaborated on Capitalism, analyzed the exploitation of surplus wealth and surplus value in industrial capitalism from many angles and concluded that they are the creation of workers and should belong to them. He asked that all the workers should unite and build socialism all over the world. He declared moral support for many movements. The world was different before the propositions of Marx and Engels and after that, the world was different. Revolutions took place under the leadership of Lenin in Russia and Mao in China, applying the proposals of Marx and Engels to the conditions of their country. Many experiments were done to establish socialist systems. Revolutions took place in many countries with the theories of Marx and Engels. They lost in some places. They succeeded in many places. Thus a socialist world was taking shape. The works of Marx and Engels worked as a basis for them. They have made many proposals in politics and movements from time to time. Lenin and Mao Granci also made many such proposals and tried to establish new governments. Gramsci's ideas remained propositions. Many others advanced in the light of Marx, Engels and the Communist Manifesto. They wrote extensively. Marxism expanded its perspective in all sciences. It is necessary to know the basic works of such people. Many have heard the names of books like Socialism, Communism, Marx, Engels, Communist Manifesto, Capital. Very few have studied the basic texts of Marxism. So let me briefly introduce the basic texts of Marxism.

Basic Marxist Texts:
1. Communist Manifesto
2. German Ideology
3. Anti-During
4. Dialectics of Nature
5. The Family as Personal Property - The Birth of the Kingdom (This is a review of Morgan's study of Native American tribes as an ancient society)
6. Ludwig Feuer Bau-German Philosophical Compendium
7. Lessons of the Paris Commune
8. Capital (alienation of capital labour-power surplus value)

Marxism - Socialism

9. Kinetic materialism, Kinetic historical materialism (based on Morgan's 'archaic society' research...primitive commune system then slave system then feudalism then capitalist industrial system then the socialist system was proposed and then the communist system\

10. Darwin's attempt to apply his formulations of nature and evolution to social systems.

11. Marx and Engels wrote that the first socialist revolutions and working class revolutions will come in Germany, England and France where the industrial revolution was successful.

12. Socialism will come all over the world at once, in chronological order Socialism was proposed to trans-form into Communism.

13. They said that the dictatorship of the proletariat under the leadership of the proletariat is necessary. Inevitable said.

14. Lenin theorized that the working class is not only the workers but that anyone with working class consciousness can become a working class and lead the working class. Working class party formulated that labor revolution is not possible without it. It was said that anyone can act as a working class with the consciousness of the working class and can lead the working class itself. Thus the middle class intellectuals propagated their national revolutions in the respective countries as Marxist working class revolutions. They tried to head towards it. Marx Engels Lenin Mao can be cited for this.

These are basically the basic works of Marx and Engels. The essence of all these is called Marxism.

In philosophy, Marx and Engels studied Plato, Aristotle, Kant, Hegel, Peure, Darwin, Morgan and other historical evolutionary philosophies well. The London Library was explored by them. Thereafter only B.R. Ambedkar alone explored the London library after many thousands of books were added to the library. Marx's philosophy and logic are mixed. It was inherited from their teacher, Hegel. It is necessary to analyze the logic in the philosophy and the philosophy in the logic. Many fell under the spell of Marx and Engels' new researches and failed to notice the mistakes made.

B.S Ramulu

Marxism ideologically triumphed all over the world:

Marxism was ideologically successful all over the world. A victory in a war does not mean that there are no flaws. Analyzing even the mistakes made after a war victory is useful in many ways.

The positivists of Marxism have thoroughly justified and analyzed. Contrary to that, Marxism bowed its neck to the opposing elements and was distorted. They refused to see the truth. Those who think differently from Marxism pointed out the flaws and opposed the philosophy and logic of Marxism but could not accept its strengths and new elements. Indeed, the practice of Marxism faced many failures. There are still many failures. In Russia and China, the system known as socialism was replaced by capitalist and democratic systems. A mixed economy was established. So, the socialist system experiments proposed by Marxism turned into a mixed economy after decades. Soviet countries were formed as Soviet Union in 1918 and split into 13 countries in 1985 and became democracies. It is a consequence of political.movements. These have their roots in Marxist philosophy and political economics. By looking at them it is made clear that many efforts were made to build a humane society.

A fundamental error has occurred.

A fallacy took place while borrowing fundamental philosophical propositions from Marx and Hegel. Marx and Engels could not recognize its importance in the conditions of society that was boiling like a volcano of that time. Even Lenin, Stalin, Mao and others could not observe the same tendency. As a result, Marxism as a practical science, political and social movement, and the one-sided tendencies in the formulation of programs have continued.

Sublation of negation by Hegel:

Hegel emphasizes the word 'negation' very well. He also emphasized sublation just as strongly. Negation means the old goes away and the new comes in, Sublation means the old continues and the new comes into being.

Morgan's findings.

Morgan wrote a book of hundreds of pages called 'Ancient Society' and did the most extensive research ever done by anyone in the world. It is about human evolution. Based on Morgan's findings, Engels wrote about analysis of the family system and the birth of the kingdoms.

Marxism - Socialism

Morgan, Darwin, Engels Formulations:

Darwin studied the evolution of nature and wrote the science of evolution. Both of these are excellent findings. Hegel's negation appears as an element of Darwin's research. Morgan wrote a large review of Engels' Family System, State, and Birth, adopting elements and formulations of ancient society. It is in circulation as a book. 'The evolution of the family, from the primitive society, from the tribal society, and the way developments took place in the family system due to the means of production and the forces of production' he explained clearly. Darwin's principle of survival of the fittest became very popular. Circumstances that change themselves only survive. Whatever does not change, perishes in nature. Darwin thus formulated that dinosaur and the like became extinct.

In this way, Marx and Engels drew the points of Morgan and Darwin and some principles of Hegel's philosophy and synthesized them.

Negation Sublation:

Another aspect of Hegel's saying that there is old and there is new is forgotten to be adopted in this coordination. This error continued to exist in the in Marxist philosophy, in logic, in kinetic materialism, historical materialism, most influential capital text of the Communist manifesto, the new proposals of World Socialism and Communism. The same error is directly encountered in political programs. This error still haunts the proponents and detractors of Marxism around the world.

Many sciences that came before Marx were accepted, rejected and critically accepted as far as they could see. If the philosophers who came after had done all the research and analysis done by Marx and made their new proposals, Marxism, philosophy, political sciences, capital family, state, birth, historical materialism, kinetic materialism etc. would have been wonderfully enriched. This work is not done. For politics, the Marxist philosophy of capital was advanced in those countries as the lessons of the French Revolution. They came to power in countries like Russia and China. After they came to power, they propagated them even more.

Survival of the Fittest – Darwin's Principle:

Chameleon is thought to be a remnant of dinosaurs. As the dinosaurs perished, the rest continued to transform themselves. Animals, birds, plants and insects have been gradually changing themselves following the changes in nature. Humans have also been changing and changing their body structure and brain to suit the conditions. It became a special science and was named as anthropology. Thus, one science has expanded into many sciences.

One thought into many sciences...:

One logic, one philosophy flows into many sciences. This way, Hegel's philosophy and logic flowed in the written chapters of Marx. Marx only took negation from Hegel. Sublation was not taken. Thus, in all works of morphism in capitals, sublation is lacking in analysis. They could not say that while the old remains dormant, the new continues. The proposals of World Socialism and World Communism were built on that flaw.

Lenin's New Chapters:

After the failure of the 1905 revolution, Lenin studied philosophies extensively in secret life. Many new proposals and understandings came to his mind. They are not discussed as complete sciences. He wrote down the things he observed in the same books. They were published in the Soviet Union as Lenin's Philosophical Notebooks in Volume 35. In it, Hegel wrote that without understanding logic and philosophy, no one in the capitalist world would understand it after 50 years. And elsewhere it is written that relationship is more fundamental than conflict. As long as there is a relation, the contradiction between the two is the unity of opposites, evolutionary change, qualitative change, negation, sublation, negation of negation, sublation of negation. But, even today there are Marxists and anti-Marxists in the world. Both camps argue that the contradiction is the main one. Without relation, there can be no contradiction. I have written about this in more detail in 1991 in the book "Nenu Kyi Gatitarka Tatva-darsabhumika".

Precedence of Sublation:

Sublation can be said to mean evolution. The science of evolution refers to evolution where the old remains and the new grows. Negation like a revolution. It can be said that as the old is gone and the new is coming. Both evolution and revolution are interdependent. Evolution

Marxism - Socialism

can lead to qualitative change. As evolution unfolds, the minority becomes the majority. The plant becomes a great tree. Babies evolve into humans and adults. The river, which started as a small channel, has expanded into a living being by joining many streams and tributaries. The sublation left by Marx and Engels in philosophy and logic will not cease to exist in the world! The world does not disappear if we close our eyes and do not recognize it. Survival of the fittest continues throughout the world following Darwin's theory of survival of the fittest. Capitalism thus transforms itself and continues to sublation.

Sublation, Evolution of varna system, caste system as sublation:
Evolution of caste system and varna system as sublation. Varna system, caste system and Brahmanism which were born like that, continue to change and mold themselves and continue like the liquid that takes the shape of the vessel in which it is poured. Capitalism itself continues to morph itself fluidly into many new roles. And so it continues and finally in socialism, in Russia and China, the capitalist system is returning to the state capitalist system and gradually to the mixed capitalist system.

While being old, the emergence of several generations:
While the tree is still there, we see the seeds germinate and many generations of new trees are born. Humans also continue as sublations up to five generations. Apart from that, negation does not end when people meet new people. Further, it can be observed that the care for loved ones is seen in the cattle, birds, animals and humans. Abandoning these laws of nature, historical materialism and kinetic materialism advanced. The main reason for this is that Hegel took negation, negation of negation from logic and left out sublation. So that one-eye vision replaces two-eye vision. Left view. The leftist vision continues.

Flaws forgotten in the triumph of Marxism:
In this way, Marxism in its various forms advanced with advanced thinking, ignoring many of the sciences of that time. Victorious, it changed the world. Human society forgets to correct errors in pride of victory. A capitalist society like America is reasserting itself because of the blind opposition and implicit following of some. Lenin idealized the American way of working, saying that the Bolshevik spirit was the American way of working. But the continuation of the

errors of Marxism in the Bolshevik spirit left the American style of work as the Soviet Union evolved into a capitalist democracy.

Taking the fundamental texts and formulations of Marxism as a guide, which were built with a one-sided view of philosophy and logic, Lenin wrote some propositions and texts that are necessary for Marxism while discussing his experiences, local conditions and changing developments while working in Russia for the socialist revolution.

1. By writing the book 'Capitalism at the highest stage of imperialism', the capitalist system expanded to the countries of the world as imperialism by the exploitation people of other areas by the non-industrial people and increasing the facilities for the workers and corrupting them.

By going against emperor Tsar that the revolutions should be successful at the weakest link of capitalist society and feeling that the socialist revolution is possible only in a weak capitalist society, and it is not possible to have socialist revolutions all over the world at the same time. He wrote that it is possible to have a socialist society, socialist government and socialist system in each country. Thus, the Russian Revolution was successful and Soviet Union became the Soviet Union in 1918 and provided an inspiration and guidance to other countries.

Those who accept these ideas of Lenin are called Marxists and Leninists. Lenin's basic texts are also required to be read. They are

1. The 14th volume of Lenin's anthologies 'Emperio Criticism and Materialism'
2. 'Lenin's Philosophical Notebooks', 38th supplemen-tary volume
3. The above mentioned 'imperialism is the highest stage of capitalism. A revolution will succeed in weak capitalist countries rather than in developed capitalist countries.
4. Kingdom - Revolution. Whenever fighting against the kingdom. Instead of weakening, the kingdom is getting stronger. Some proposals have been made in this that after the revolution is successful, the existing government systems, employees, teachers, workers and farmers will be trained according to the

Marxism - Socialism

socialist goals and will be suitably adapted towards the public interest.

5. The Duma (Parliament runs with numbers after winning the election, important among Lenin's formulations after running for the Duma and winning.

6. There is no working-class revolution without a working-class party, and we must form our own armed forces. Another basic formulation was made that a working-class party is not necessarily a party built with workers, anyone who works with working class consciousness is a working-class person and becomes a working class party.

Due to this Leninist formulation middle class writers, artists, intellectuals, petty bourgeoisie, and those who came from the rich peasantry like Puchchalapalli Sundarayya, Ravi Narayana Reddy, Bhimreddy Narsimha Reddy, Charmajumdar and finally Marx, Engels, Lenin, Mao would be accepted as working-class, working-class party leaders, working class perspective Marxists, working class benefactors.

Therefore, if Leninism is not accepted, no one but the workers can think of themselves as the leadership and representatives of working-class Marxism, the working-class party, or have the right to speak and work.

Therefore, many people who speak, write, work and agitate in working class parties around the world are not from the working class, but from the middle-class intellectuals, from other groups, especially from the petty bourgeoisie and rich peasant groups.

1. Mao said that after the revolution of the Soviet Union, a socialist revolution can be made in China as well. In China, which is an agrarian society, the bourgeoisie should bring about an industrial revolution involving the workers, the working-class party, the petty bourgeoisie, the middle class and other sections, up to the national bourgeoisie, together with the peasantry. Because it comes under the leadership of the working class, it is New Democracy. It is proposed that the revolution is a people's democratic revolution.

As the government continues under the leadership of the working class, the bourgeois industrial revolution or the mass democratic revolution can be peacefully transformed into a socialist revolution without the need for another revolution.

2. In their country, which is a rural and agricultural society, they formulated the need for a 'new democratic revolution' that includes everyone, where everyone including the national bourgeoisie has the opportunity to grow, to work to speed up the industrial revolution by mobilizing the rural system. Those who accept this are called Maoists, Naxalites and Maoists.

These are Mao's basic works and propositions. 1. Practice, 2. Contradictions Essays. However, in the 1970s comparative criticism emerged from the Soviet Union that these two chapters of textbooks in the Soviet Union were written giving examples of the Chinese movement. The formation of the armed forces, the slogans and formations of establishing state power through the barrel of a gun are Mao's basic ideas. Another fundamental formulation was that it was necessary and possible to make a working class out of the peasantry.

In the name of Marxism, some formulations have been made in addition to the specific conditions of the time and place by incorporating the movements and their experiences in the respective countries. Some accepted them. Some disagreed. Some stop at Marx, some stop at Lenin, some stop at Mao. Their contemporaries and colleagues in those periods formulated many aspects different from their formulations. But they are not in power. Those in power have translated them into world languages on behalf of the respective governments.

For example, we have not received the texts and lessons written by the Blanquists who revolutionized the Paris Commune. But Marx and Engels, who criticized the revolution as unwanted, an action of haste and not needed, after the success of the Paris proletariat revolution and the overthrow of the Paris Commune for two months by a military conspiracy, owned it more than those who made that revolution, and said "If we don't have our own army, the army of bourgeois governments will come to power and overthrow the commune", a new formulation was developed that the working class party should have its own army.

It has been an important formulation in practice throughout the world since the Russian Revolution. Thus the aim was to build an

Marxism - Socialism

armed force to counter the military conspiracy with an armed Red Army. Thus, under the leadership of the working-class party, the most important thing which has come forward is to create its own armed forces from the people to achieve state power. Those who come forward are engaged in armed struggle. Mao formulated this supremely as 'power through the barrel of a gun' and turned it into a slogan.

It is the basic formulation and structure followed by working class parties and movements. However, there are millions of intellectuals, artists, writers, scientists, philosophers and textbook producers all over the world who are using the Marxist perspective, methodology and approach in their respective fields, sciences and analyses, regardless of working-class parties and movements. They basically adopted some of the above mentioned Marxism, Leninism and Maoism. Apart from them, what others have said can also be adopted. For example, Bukharin's understanding was different from Stalin's understanding. Maybe in 1929 when Lenin died... Stalin sentenced him to death. Sometime after 1985, the membership of Soviet Bolshevik was restored and he was honored. Similarly, he disagreed with Trotsky Lenin also.

Trotsky also briefly served as a minister in Lenin's government. He said that in order for this Soviet revolution to spread all over the world as Marx said, a permanent revolution is necessary. Lenin did not agree and called it a continuous revolution. Thus there were few differences with some words and feelings. Trotsky was also executed under Stalin's leadership. Feminists within Marxists still embrace people like Rosa Luxemburg and Alexandria Kolantay who compare Bukharin, Trotsky and Lenin. And yet there are many types of Marxists.

All the experiences and practices are created from the study, experiences and practices of the respective countries, leaders and philosophers. This is indirect knowledge. And for anyone, this is indirect knowledge only. One has to achieve direct knowledge. Experiences are gained and lessons are learned through direct practice. From them direct knowledge grows newly and additionally. By examining the indirect knowledge through one's experience, one analyzes the past and combines the present knowledge as direct knowledge.

B.S Ramulu

Grancy recorded his experiences in Italy in his Prison Diary. Grancy and Dr. B.R. Ambedkar's ideas can be said to be democratic socialism or achieving socialism through democracy. The similarity between them is that they work for social justice and social change by bringing together many social groups.

Middle class in the name of working class

Lenin's formulation that everyone who works with proletarian consciousness are proletariat, laid the foundation for many distortions. According to the way a man is born, brought up and lived, it becomes clear which category he belonged in the relationship between categories. But because of Lenin's formulation, those who followed the trends of working class ideology, consciousness, talking, working or seeming to work for the self-interest of the middle class, intellectuals, educated petty bourgeoisie, bourgeoisie, rich peasants, and high positions in power, dominance and social honor, for the purpose of enjoying various privileges, all those who continue to speak and write theories and speak in the name of the working class happened to be called and categorized as the Working Class and not due to one's birth, the way one is brought up and the way of living.

The words, songs, speeches and writings of such educated people made the working class look weak and worthless, who have no assets except their wings and labor power. In the name of the working class, the petty bourgeoisie, the bourgeoisie, the rich peasants, the middle class are supported by all the ranks and groups that have grown up and are growing up through the state, through domination, through modern development. All of them together praise themselves as they are better poets, artists, writers, leaders, organizations, parties and movements with greater working-class consciousness than the working class itself. Everyone, including the media, cooperates with them. Criticizing those who come from the real working class as backward and not yet having the consciousness of the working-class consciousness due to compartmental thinking and did not come out of empiricism and continue to boast about their practicing world socialism, communism and Marxism at a universal level. They write too. They also take such forms of struggle. They talk about international robbery gangs very seriously.

They develop movements against governments and multinational private entrepreneurs in countries like America and Europe. They step

Marxism - Socialism

back when they have to move against the Local, direct exploiters and against all the hegemony of the dominants. But are ahead in the campaigning. The local direct exploiters live by doing jobs and doing chores for the owners. They dominate in the fields of theoretical field ideology, education, literature, art, culture, social, democracy and civil rights. They manage them. It looks like the fiction writing of Kodavatiganti Kutumbarao called Violence and Ahimsa. One who is fat emphasizes the need for non- violence and the one who is thin emphasizes the necessity of violence. While both of them argue with each other, the fat one who says non-violence is important strangles the thin one who says emphasizes violence. In India, those who are in the position of privilege in the social honors of the petty bourgeoisie, those who are living by taking part in modern development, rich farmers, writers, artists, intellectuals and leaders, suppress the voice and leadership of the real working class and come forward as the real working-class consciousness.

For decades, educated people, intellectuals, petty bourgeois rich farmers and the middle class have paraded as the working class in India. According to Lenin's principle, anyone who works with working class consciousness is a working-class person. This way, those who came from non-working class do not let the working class rise, and leading as working class and opposing those who are rising from the real working class. On the other hand, in philosophy, it is said that there is no class for others except class in itself and class for itself. When class for itself comes from a class, it is limited to the interests of that class. It means to live. Neither the middle class, nor the educated, nor the intellectuals, nor the efforts made for the working class is 'class for itself'. Class for Others means altruism. Class for Others is to serve those who are not of one's class, caste, and region with humanitarian values. This word of altruism has been going on since before Buddha. But, in Marxist philosophical debates, the term "class for others" has been ruthlessly condemned and opposed. In fact, Marx, Engels, Lenin, Mao etc. did not come from the working class. With a humanitarian perspective, they worked for the interests of the working class from being in the capitalist class, the intellectual class, the middle class. Class for others, altruism, if not accepted, would be to say that human society is frozen. Change was not possible due to the frozen categories, caste and color system. As they evolve and expand towards philanthropy and humanitarian values, the movement of classes moves towards the evolution of classes.

Marx, Engels, Lenin and Mao who came from the educated class sometimes behaved in this way towards the leader-ship from the working class and pushed them back by calling them as empiricism, sectarianism, trade unionism, militant economic-ism and various names to suit the occasion. They hit back at the other's argument with their argument only.

While Pravudhan wrote 'philosophy of poverty', they counter attacked as 'poverty of philosophy'. Other socialists were criticized as utopia socialists. They described theirs as Scientific Socialism. In fact, this scientific socialism is logical socialism achieved logically, not scientific socialism but logical socialism. Anything can be proved by reaching a logical conclusion. It is enough to know the logic. By logic presupposed, void is created, and in that void, proposition is established as a synthesis. By the time of Acharya Nagarjuna this science of logic was highly developed. This logic has been studied as a science since the fifth century BC at Taxila University. He said that the workers and leaders who came from the working class were stuck in empiricism and in the truth of the militant trade union of the working class. Ultimately, he concluded that political consciousness is the decisive factor. On this occasion it is necessary to discuss it from another angle.

When it is said that it is possible for someone with political consciousness to become working class consciousness, to work, to lead movements, to work in the fields of ideology, theory, literature and art, then it is absurd to say that there is only a class in itself, a class for itself. The saying that anyone can become working class with working class consciousness confirms that any class can change into another class with its own consciousness.

So what should we call it when it is possible to change from one category to another? That is generally called altruism. If it is theorized, it will be a class for others. Buddha and many others said to serve, sacrifice and love one's fellows with altruism, love and compassion. Buddha also gave this advice to kings. That is, the king should rule in favor of the people, evolving from the nature of his ruling class. This is possible only when it becomes a class for others.

Marxism - Socialism

Emperor Ashoka thus worked hard to spread Buddhism throughout the world. The same applies to any Marxists who say that he did this for his administration. Marxism, like Ashoka, was born for the global expansion of the ideas and leadership of the industrialized countries of Europe in the name of working-class consciousness of their ideology. Also expanded. Therefore, it is nothing but European hegemony. Because the countries of Europe looted and oppressed the countries of Asia, Africa, Australia, Red Indian and America and moved the natural resources and human resources and achieved industrial development. Marx, Engels and Marxism could not say that the looted wealth should be sent back to the respective countries and the respective countries should mobilize for that.

Since the societies that have fallen behind industrial development due to this European exploitation, they could not say that they want to grow on their own and the backward people, societies, production forces of those countries should fight against the developed European countries, achieve their own local domestic industrial development, science and technology, and make new discoveries following their historical heritage of science and technology. On the contrary, they proposed that the capitalist class should grow and capitalist industrial development should expand and spread throughout the world, so that the working class like the working class in Europe and the capitalist like capitalist class will grow. Like Emperor Ashoka propagated Buddhism for philanthropy, Marxism propagated its Europe-centrism of capitalism, industrial revolution to create the relations of production and the emerging classes in other countries as well. Proposed too. Strategy, moves, programs, slogans all brought this forward. The implication of the slogan "Workers of the world is united" is that capitalist industrial development throughout the world, capitalists, and the working class should develop in the same way. Dr|| Rammanohar Lohia discussed this matter at length and emphasized that production methods and production relations should be based on human resources and natural resources in Asian countries and there is no need for machines, science and technology that can make human resources jobless through mechanization. Therefore, he proposed that Buddhism is class for self, class for others benevolence, love, compassion, wisdom, Buddha is sheltered by Buddha, Dhamma is sheltered by God, Sangam is sheltered by community. . For centuries the world has been driven forward by the guidelines of living with love and compassion while accepting and practicing society, dharma and wisdom. Ultimately, these ideals will continue in tomorrow's society as well.

But the non-working class ranks and groups who pass themselves off as Marxists in the name of working-class consciousness denigrate others. They strongly argue that that they are the ones who move the society forward, that everyone should follow their leadership, and that the state power should be under their leadership. In the personal practice the arrogance of landlords, rich farmers and police would continue. Thus the personal pride and supremacy is masked by working class consciousness. It is also theorized that it is a leadership trait and character. They criticize all the people who should be together and keep them away from being together in their organizations and movements and say that they are not coming together again.

They behave as if they mock with their foreheads and laugh with their mouths. What makes all this possible for them? This is made possible by the formulation that anyone can become working class with working class consciousness. Where were they born? Where did you grow up? What is their way of life? What is their culture? What is their relative class? What is their place in the forces of production, means of production, relations of production, distribution of production, hegemony? Are they in a dominant position? Are they among the producers? Are they descended from those who continued to be parasitic classes in feudal relations of production? Are they the ones who came as teachers for alienation? Are they descended from the petty bourgeoisie who have been enjoying the relations of production and production without participating in the capitalist society? Are they descended from the petty bourgeoisie who are being alienated and exploited by participating in production?

They can be called as Small-scale farmers, peasant labourers, small-scale artisans, cottage industries and small-scale modern industrial producers are the petty bourgeoisie who participate in production and are alienated and exploited. What are their allies in the ruling classes and the exploited classes in the social sphere? What are natural ally groups that cooperate even if they don't want to? What are the additional benefits and leadership positions they are getting? By

Marxism - Socialism

leaving them unexamined, they circulate themselves as working-class, working-class writers, artists, intellectuals, philosophers and leaders.

By cooperating outside of the class they came from, the petty bourgeois who are not related to the supply, who are enjoying dominance over production, production and services, are able to grow as leaders, artists, intellectuals and civil rights activists by cooperating from outside the class they came from. Those from the genuine working class, alienated and exploited communities are pushed back by lack of such opportunities. I have specifically analyzed how this happens and what the order is in the stories of Politics, Mother's breast milk, Dakshayagna, Jeevanyanam, etc.

In this way, the educated, the middle class, the intellectuals and even the petty bourgeoisie are not a class. These are different categories from non-productive sectors. This is a category. Another category comes from the middle class, the petty bourgeoisie, who are involved in production, alienated and exploited. These two are not the same. Those who come from the productive sectors are working class consciousness. Direct knowledge and direct practice belong to them.

Non-productive class have indirect knowledge. If those from the non-productive classes dominate those from the forces of production, it is the domination of other classes over the working class. Other classes, dominant castes, dominant castes and dominant classes continue to exercise power in the name of the working class. This can be observed from Marx and Engels themselves since the birth of Marxism throughout the world. This is what intellectuals say is Marxism. They have split into hundreds of parties arguing and practicing that the revolution they say is the truth and the programs they say are true. The call to unite workers of the world has finally been reduced to 'walk with us'. Different groups were created.

Thus the working classes from the forces of production, the workers who work with the means of production, are different from the educated and the petty bourgeoisie from the non- productive sectors. One comes from the classes alienated from the ruling classes, from the dominant classes, from the dominant castes, while the other comes from the working classes, the forces of production, the sparks that work directly with the means of production, the alienated from the ruled. Thus, these two types of conflicts, class conflict and caste conflict between the middle class, the intellectuals, the educated, and the petty bourgeoisie continue continuously. It is said that there will be a friendly conflict between these two middle class petty bourgeois groups and it should be resolved as a friendly conflict. But in reality, in practice one can see the continuing order of hegemons who come from the upper castes, the rich peasantry, the capitalists, and those who come from the rest of the proletariat, the working class.

Thus educated people from non-productive, dominant sectors continue to be left-wing and dominant. If they are not dominant, they will exit. They continue to be limited to their interests.

It is very difficult to bear them in the respective movements and parties. It is like living in the same family and enduring domestic violence, these relationships continue as the wife is constantly abused by the husband. It is accepted that the dominance of the Educated petty-bourgeois from the upper castes, is as natural as the patriarchal dominance and is culturally accepted.

Due the gap between the castes, it is natural for those who come from the upper caste to dominate more easily. The educated and middle class have not discussed this polemic for decades and they talk as if the petty bourgeoisie are all one class. That is very wrong. Those who come from wealthy backgrounds may have more knowledge. Due to the support of their social groups and castes around them, they may become leaders in many fields. All this serves to push the labor class, their leadership and the leadership of the working classes. It can be observed at every stage in India for hundreds of years. Generally, such people take advantage of the castes, communities, relatives, their positions, their positions in the society, through their relations with them. It gives them unique opportunities. From this arose the argument of organic intellectuals. They are called womb geniuses. Subaltern theories, Subaltern Studies, Kanche Ilayya, K. S. Chalam, Kathi Padmarao and others like me put forward the importance of Garbhastha Medha. We also refer to this as Bhumi Putrulu, Son of the Soil. In the last few decades, 75 percent of the industrialists and wealthy people in America have grown from the first generation of intellectuals. The character of the first generation of Garbhastha Madhevas and their skills can be seen with this example. Even in India when first generation intellectuals are given these opportunities, 75

Marxism - Socialism

percent of the first generation will grow up from intellectuals, educated, laborers, BC, SC, ST, castes.

Even in feminism, feminism of the working class, feminism of the middle class and the intellectuals has been continuing in two special ways. Feminists have been proving and confirming for several decades that Marxism is basically a theory and practice dominated by patriarchal ideologies. By not considering women's labor, labor power, and production in discussions of the added value of capital labor capitalism and economics in Marxism remained half a science. It can be said according to the formulation of feminists that it has become a half-truth. Moreover, science, technology, achievements of scientists, inventions, gains and benefits achieved with management skills are basically the added value of the working class in Marxism. This is a misconception. From this mistaken opinion, since everything is the creation of the workers and everything should belong to the workers, they came to the formulation of a labor dictatorship. In fact, the industrial revolution was accelerated by the inventions made by scientists. As innovations have been made in many fields, many ranks and categories like engineers, scientists, workers, managers have been increasing in the construction of systems in all fields.

The discovery of electricity, the discovery of radio waves, the discovery of photography, and the discovery of cinema led millions of people to new fields. These are all different, skilled services, industries and marketing approaches than the textile mill workers who came first. The labor power of the ploughmen is greater with plowshares. The labor force of those who dig and plow with tractor and JCB is less. The result is more. All this result is not the result of the worker, it has a great contribution from the inventions of scientists. This is called intellectual property in recent times. All the inventions of science and technology belong to the entire humanity. Therefore, having created enough wealth for the employment of workers and the development of living standards, the rest of the surplus value and surplus wealth should belong to the human society. The same is the contribution of experts and scientists. Therefore, the argument that all the wealth is only created by workers is invalid. The argument of working-class dictatorship based on it is also invalid. It can be seen here that if a company runs in profits, it is due to the workers and if there is a loss, it is due to the lack of ownership. It is some-thing like the profit is mine and the loss is yours. The impor-tance of management skills is evident here.

Earlier, Brahmins were respected as Bhusuras, equal to God, as God is Mantradhinam, Mantra is Brahmandhinam, Brahman is Mamadevata. Society is led by the working-class leadership. Working class consciousness is working class leadership. Therefore, the working-class party is defined as the working class as Brahman or Mamadevata. They said that there is no working-class revolution without a working-class party. In this way, the party is said to be the working class as the Brahmin and God have become heroes in a logical order.

So what is the need to bring the real working class into leadership? Whoever comes from Marxism mantras become Marxists, working class and working-class leadership, just as the Brahmin who got the mantras through Marxism ideology, consciousness and practice becomes equal to God and God. The roots of the educated, petty-bourgeois people coming from the rich classes and the upper castes to talk that they are the working class and that they are the leadership of the working class are in the formulation that God is mantra, mantra is Brahman, Brahman is Mother Goddess. Therefore, Lenin's definition of the working-class party and its workers has become the principle of God's control. It is because of this formulation that no matter what class they come from, no matter what kind of life they lead, Marxist mantras come, so they are all worshiped as Marxist gods. Party supremacy should be in all spheres, centralized democratic leadership i.e. Brahmin or Mama Deva, as the unquestionable supreme authority that dictates, defines and defines various and they feel a level of dominance in nests and compartments. They command others to submit to it and respect their status. Herein lies the roots of the arrogant display of Marxists' ideological discourse. These are related to landlordism, thought policing and police third degrees. They are said to have changed the form and essence of Marxism. But their form and essence is hegemony. A place that alienates all but is not separate.

In Lenin's book 'Revolutionary Revolution', when the question of what to do with the existing government employees after the revolution came, it was said that they should be trained in the Bolshevik spirit. I must have read the book 'Kingdom Revolution' at least 50 times. Even after the revolution, they are the employees, they

Marxism - Socialism

are the teachers, they are in all the fields, then what did the people do the revolution for, just to come to power in the name of the party leaders and the working class? I thought so. Why leave the government job and do movements. I thought seriously. Is it only few people who understood this 'Rajyam Viplavam' book so deeply. It is not easy to understand. Those who leave their existing jobs and work at lower levels without any leadership can understand its pain and suffering. Noting the error in Lenin's opinion, I wrote an article that when the revolution came in Nepal, everyone who worked in the revolution should be given government jobs, policemen, soldiers, and laborers and given skills training in all fields. Why did Lenin make that formulation? The reason why he did it was that he also came from such educated and intellectual class. So, he made such a suggestion. If he came from the working class, the first generation of educated people, if he came from the first generation of intellectuals, there was no possibility of making that formulation.

Priority was given to making new generations, from new generations, leaving aside the existing employees and teachers. The Bolsheviks encouraged the old to take voluntary retirement and work in other areas of life and leisure. Because Lenin did not come from the working class, he came from the educated and intelligentsia, after the revolution, he spoke of the dictatorship of the working class, neglected the workers, prioritized the educated and intellectuals in the fields that were available at that time, led the story, and took up new structures. In the same order, as two generations passed, they pushed the working class back and rose into all fields as capitalists, bureaucrats, politicians, and working-class leaders, and eventually the workers removed the feelings of priority and dominance and came back to a mixed economy in the name of public welfare. This is how the middle-class intellectuals came to power. Over time, the working classes pushed it back and established their state power. This is what happened in China, even through Mao. It is strange that Mao insists that there is no class in itself, class for others. Because philanthropy in China and Asian countries, Buddhism and other religions also promoted philanthropy as a great human value. Mao, who came from such a heritage, said that there is no class for others. In other words, Mao also turned the revolution in favor of the interests of the middle class educated and intellectuals and established their leadership.

B.S Ramulu

Mao said a great thing. He said that in order to mobilize a movement to change a village one has to study hundred years of history. But the three generations of those who circulate as this working class are brothers, sisters, blood relations, friendship relations, attachments, classmates, colleagues, etc. are kept hidden. They take care. In this way, they hide all the factors that affect their class nature and try to look like working class consciousness.

How to declass from that class and to what extent it happened to decast? So, what should be checked to certify as decast and declassed? Who should check? Are they from the same petty-bourgeois section who beat their own cans by calling themselves the working class and Marxists?

Or the ones those in agricultural and cottage industry societies for centuries, in the forces of production, or the owners of that day? Or the working-class activists from the classes of producers, servants, the oppressed and the ruling classes? Who should check?

At present, for decades in India, the educated petty bourgeoisie, rich farmers, landlords, and those from the middle class have been dominant as the leadership of the working class, and they themselves have been deciding who is the working-class consciousness, who is decast and declassed, and what it means to be decast and declassed. In this way, those who came from the sections that had experienced the lion's share in the domination of the petty-bourgeoisie, royalist, agrarian societies, cottage industries and production relations continue to circulate as the working class and as the leadership of Marxism. In this way, the real working class, the real rulers and the oppressed classes are being prevented from growing into the leadership of the working class by standing in the way and closing the doors. Something like when you cannot ask someone to leave, create a situation that is untenable for them to stay. Whatever they say, they insist that it is alien ideology, empiricism, and self-centeredness. That is why they are excelling in other fields except working class consciousness organizations and movements and are not being allowed to grow as the leaders of the working class who direct those fields except as flag bearers and activists.

Since the time of Mahatma Jyoti Rao Phule, for 160 years, there have been continuous movements with the conscious-ness of the

Marxism - Socialism

working class. In literature, in stories, in novels, in films, neither the level of those movements nor the level of leadership of the Left camp parties that led them were depicted. Why did this happen? If all the left- wing writers like Prem Chand and Kishan Chander wrote about the working-class people, why are they not seen in literature, art and cinema? Stories and novels about Singareni coal mine workers did not come in to light until the workers themselves became conscious and wrote about the working class themselves.

No matter how much those coming from upper caste petty bourgeoisie say that they are working class consciousness, their roots and limitations are in the class related to the caste they were born and brought up in, the job they are currently working in, the life they are experiencing and living. That is why, instead of writing about the workers, they are writing it as a fiction about their friends, grandchildren, great-grand-children, daughters, neighbors, relatives and auquaintances by only responding to them. Therefore, they are Marxists in words, petty bourgeois in deeds and life. They have become a hindrance to the growth of real working-class leadership in all spheres. Therefore, it is inevitable that pro-people, true working-class consciousness should come forward in other forms by questioning and opposing those who circulate in the name of Left Camp and the left ideology that they use as their weapons.

Who are the leaders of those movements? How do they work?

How their hundreds of years of heritage class natures and developments continue? It is inevitable to oppose the circulation of working class and Left Camp leaders without examining their roots. The more it expands, the more it means that the real working class is emerging as a working class. As much class struggle and ideological struggle is done against the petty bourgeoisie who have been dominant in the relations of production for centuries; social justice, social change and leadership position will be possible for the petty bourgeoisie who came from the production sectors, from the oppressed classes and the working class.

Kinetic Logic - Kinetic Philosophy

Gati means motion. Kinetics is the process of intuiting and uncovering the nature of movement, mutual effects, nature, and thus changing patterns in things, society, and human relationships. The translation of kinetic logic to dialectics (is it correct, kindly check) does not give the correct meaning. Translated as 'Gati Tattva'is correct. Teaching and sensing the motion of the respective objects is kinetic philosophy. When it is extracted from nature, it is called kinetic logical materialism, and when it examines the processes of social evolution, it is called historical materialism.

The program to bring out those movements and to implement them presently is called Marxism strategy, moves and program. Also known as Ambedkarism's strategy, moves and programme. Kinetic logic is to find out the principles of motion and the order of evolution in an object, society, production relations and human relations. Moreover, to extract and analyze according to kinetic logic and its principles is like a juggler putting a rabbit in a hole and taking out the rabbit again saying that he changed a man into rabbit.

This is what you thought but it is not a revelation of the contradictions in the object, the unity between the contra-dictions, their clash, evolutionary and qualitative changes. Kinetic logic is the discovery of patterns of motion in their nature.

Kinetics basically means to find out and extract the true nature of the object and then taking programs according to their preferences. In this calculation, the nature of the object should be seen as the same for everyone. Manifested in various ways means that the object has different sides and patterns of motion. So they are all different aspects of that object. If all of them are combined, it is possible to know the complete sequence of motion of the object.

Metaphysics is called so, because the nature of motions and sequences in an object by breaking their interrelationships and examination. When examined in their mutual natures, in the movement of mutual relations, in the unity of opposites, in their conflict, it is called dialectics.

For example the Greek philosopher Zeno made a discussion. An arrow is always motionless at any given fraction of second during its journey. That is why he said that the arrow is not moving. 24 frames are fixed in a film reel. At 24 frames per second they appear to be moving. The entire film seems to move with static frames like this. This is how Geno's proposition that the arrow is not moving should be understood. Time is missing in this. Breaking each second apart

Marxism - Socialism

will cause the arrow not to move. The film reel frames are not moving. This can be called metaphysics. This formulation was arrived at due to the severing of the relationship between time and space.

It is true that the arrow moves if the relationship between the space and time is established. This is kinetic logic. i.e. understanding motion sequences.

Lenin wrote a word in his philosophical notebooks. While studying Hegel's kinetic logic... "However, it is said that Marx wrote Capital applying Hegel's kinetic theory to political economy. From this calculation, Lenin opined that if one reads Capital without understanding Hegel's kinetic logic, no one will understand it after 50 years.

What did Hegel say in kinetic logic? Applying it to political economy and analyzing how Marx wrote Capital, analyzing and researching Capital, and balancing them both only would be understanding Marx and Capital.

When human relations, production relations, social and political relations, natural developments are separated from their interrelationships, they arrive at the metaphysical argument that the arrow does not move (like the frames of a movie reel). Buddha said that objects change in mutual relations. This is known as 'Pratitya Samutpada'. Kinetic logic in Buddhism examines multiple causes and relationships rather than a single cause.

It is not Marxism to say that according to Marxism this should be done and that should be done. Those who say so are not Marxists. Engels repeated this saying over and over again. It means that such people consider motions as inert and inert.

Society is not inert. Many human relationships keep continuing. They are constantly in motion and mutually influencing each other and are changing. When they are conceived in the order of those motions and relations, it becomes dynamism, and would result into extraction of the principles of primordial motions. Engels insisted on this study.

These are fundamental elements of the dynamic philosophy of Marxism. If these are known and discovered through direct knowledge from time to time in the present, it becomes kinetic philosophy. When added with the proposition that the working class will lead to a socialist system by creating some programs accordingly, it becomes a political program of Marxism.

Investment, Labour, Value Added:

Capital, labour, surplus value is also a theory of Knowledge. Accumulation from the past is investment. All indirect knowledge is accumulated by human society with its practice and thought. Thus investment is the accumulation, wealth, savings of the surplus value of erstwhile labor power of human society. It participates in the creation of surplus value along with existing labor force. Labor power is the thing of present. Investment is the thing of past. Indirect knowledge is a thing of the past. Direct knowledge, direct practice is the thing of present. No new knowledge or additional knowledge can be created as 'added value' without the laborious effort of direct practice.

Implicit knowledge is the accumulation, investment of knowledge acquired by Society.

It has to be said that Marx's basic research on investment, about accumulation of past knowledge and adding it to labor power and investment is wrong if additional knowledge is not generated.

Both physical labor and mental labor are part of physical labor.

Therefore, the knowledge investment of the principles of social nature movement written by achieving morphism, with the accumulation of knowledge investment, using physical intellectual labor power, when practical direct knowledge is carried forward additional knowledge as value must be generated continuously.

Only then is it concluded that the labour-power of the worker is fundamental in the creation of surplus value.

Marxism is an investment of knowledge. When they work on it with their hard work and practice, additional knowledge and new knowledge will come from that hard work as an additional value.

It should contribute its share to the reinvestment.

Many people use the word category very often. They add the word "class" and speak and write as Classes, class perspective, oppressed classes, exploited classes, working class, capitalist class, landed class. Those who limit themselves to the word class are just babbling

Marxism - Socialism

Marxism. Those who say this is 'wrong' as per Marxism and 'right' as per Marxism are not Marxists. This is just babbling. Engels himself emphasized this point.

Marx and Engels were great human beings. They wanted the world to grow into a socialist society without exploitation. Continued with high ideals. They made some proposals from time to time in terms of strategies and moves in the design of programs. Some people focused only on these and did not study the original basic propositions. Basic propositions need to be understood following principles and theories. Marx and Engels studied German philosophers like Kant, Hegel and Fuerba in philosophy and adopted what was suitable for them.

Sublation negation:

Negation is taken from Hegel. Hegel makes two points. The first is negation, and the second is sublation. The old goes and the new comes is negation. As mentioned earlier, the old exists and new would also exist is sublation. Marx and Engels forgot to adopt this second point. A tree exists and its seeds will grow into trees again. There are grandfathers, fathers, grandmothers, grandmothers, sons, daughters-in-law, sons-in-law, grandchildren and great-grandchildren. Four generations live together. In the evolution of nature, unlike the negation of human evolution, the old remains and the new is born and continues. Over time the tree dries up. People die. Their DNA, the DNA of the plants, continues in the form of descendants, in the form of seeds. During the period of Marx, Engels, the DNA continuum was not discovered. They preferred negation. According to Hegel, the continuation of both the old and the new can be observed in the simultaneous continuation from the tribal societies to the modern societies. Marx and Engels defined social structure as classes. In this sense, Arthasastra is restructured in "Capital". The tenets of arthashastra were examined and analyzed during the very strong reconstruction.

These theories have been put into practice and some works are being done in a new formulation. When they are put back into practice, many experiences arise. New formulations will come from them. Old ones are re-evaluated from time to time. Thus, the Soviet Union and China entered into a democratic and mixed economic system. First, they said 'one-party dictatorship'. Everything should be under the government. It was called nationalization and socialism. Having found the mistakes and with experiences after some time, China must have put forward the slogan 'let some people be rich first'.

Thus by the encouragement of private industrialists and the industrial sector of the 13 countries of the Soviet Union and China with 1.5 billion population continued democratic governance with limited democratic approach.

Thus, they have gained many direct experiences in the administration of one-party dictatorship, one party administration and working-class dictatorship. Many new formulations were made from it. After independence, India has been following a mixed economy system in two ways, private indu-strial sector and government owned industrial sector. Now 13 countries of Soviet Russia, including China, have taken a turn with these administrative systems and limited democratic systems. Some of these inexperienced Marxists who cannot accept these policies, some parties do not recognize the eriences of those countries and hold old theories and formulations as if they have more experience than them and oppose the current policies. Thus some Marxists are not ready to accept the knowledge of direct experiences and their consequences. Thus, by wanting to keep and practice the ideas and theories said by Marx and Engels, they are changing them to the level of religion. Engels, Mao, and Marx took the basic points of Engels and molded them into National Socialists for the liberation of their nation and their people. Thus, observing the conditions in their countries, they made movements suitable for them. Those respective national movements can be called Russian national movement and Chinese national movement. For that, they adopted some points of Marx and Engels. After that, they again followed their own experiences and turned to new approaches and moved forward like that.

In 1985, Russia split into 13 countries. The campaign slogan 'Glasnasty Peristroica' was put forward. On the other hand, Dunkel's proposals and the GATT agreement came forward as part of global trade and commercial agreements. The countries of the world have accepted these and following. Starting from 1985 and starting from 1990, the countries of the world are going through the phase of globalization, privatization, liberalization (Liberalization, Privatization, Globalization - LPG). Now the whole world is

Marxism - Socialism

following this LPG phase. Structures, agreements, activities, relations between countries like World Bank, United Nations, World Health Organization, Brexit, T-20, SAARC are continuing. 'What are the fundamentals of Marxism at this stage?' and 'What are the programs?' are to be examined separately. Many fundamental principles of Marxism are very valuable. The programs and slogans given from time to time and the formulations made in favor of it become outdated. Lenin said "Friend! Theories and formulations become outdated. The tree of life is constantly blooming green."

Forces of production – means of production
Relations of Production – Caste Category Negotiations

The term category is a judgment in an evolution. A commentary. They are discussed with the terms like 'forces of production, means of production, relations of production, labor power, investment, surplus value, relations of distribution , hegemony, alienation, exploitation'. Accordingly, while discussing the relations of production in India, Marx stated that the rural self- sustenance economy in India had continued. It continued to be the foundation of the caste system. Let me discuss this in Marxist terms.

The forces of production in India for centuries were Shudras, Atishudras and tribals. The means of production are theirs. Production relations in the Rural Society continued as mutually self-sustaining. Varna system, caste system, karma, reincarnation theories and practices have been determining the relations of production, distribution system and its ownership. Brahmins, Kshatriyas, Vaishyas, never took part in production. They claimed Lion's share of should belong to them and directed that the above three varnas to be served by Shudras and Atishudras.

As the foundation of Varna caste systems...:

In this way, the caste system continues to alienate and exploit the production. So caste system, varna system, karma, reincarnation ideologies, ownership of relations of production and dominance as a practical consequence create categories. Thus, caste and caste system are the mother which creates categories out of relations of production. And a category is its child. Thus the relationship between caste and class is the relationship between mother and child. The caste gives birth to category.

B.S Ramulu

The word class is a judgment that emerges in the final sequence of social relations and relations of production. To talk about judgment without knowing the order is to talk without knowing the subject. So those who discuss with the word 'class' do not know the concepts of capital, forces of production, relations of production, means of production, surplus value, distributor of production, alienation, exploitation and domination in Marxism. It can be accepted that those who debate these terms may know some extent of Marxism. Moreover, it can be said that those who discuss with the words class and class perspective are using that word to only say what they want to say, and that they do not want real Marxism. The word 'class' in the discussion of caste problem, caste differences, caste discrimination, abolition of caste and relations of production means that they have no under-standing of Marxism, especially Marxist political semantics.

Therefore, those who try to preface the discussion of caste with the word class are basically those who act as if they know and do not know A, B, C and D of Marxism.

Marxism, Capital holds that the forces of production, means of production, relations of production, surplus value, distribution and alienation determine social relations. But relations of production are of two types. One is production of relations that work with nature and natural resources. The second is reproductive relationships of two human beings. Caste has been determining these two relationships for centuries. Category is a term limited only to relations of. Production Caste has two meanings and has an order. Thus caste refers to two things while category refers to only one thing. Marxism had to examine separately the reproductive relations of human beings, i.e. male and female relations, family system, child rearing, patriarchal and patriarchal social relations, and the consequences. Caste has been examining and prescribing both simultaneously. Thus category is only an interpretation. Caste is indeed an ongoing aspect of life, practice, relations of production and relations of reproduction. It is discussed as the rich and the poor. And it is not discussed in the terminology of Marxism. The ruling class, the ruled class and the exploiting class are they way they are discussed in Marxism.

Many people who talk about caste and class say that class is important. They feel that there is no category perspective in the

Marxism - Socialism

discussion of caste problem. Those who discuss whether it is caste or class, or those who talk about caste class society, should necessarily know how the word category is formed and in what sense it is used.

To oppose the issue of caste, those who oppose to recognize its importance use and the term category to argue.

Fundamentals of Marxist Political Economics

1. Forces of production
2. Means of production
3. Production relations
4. Development of science and technology
5. Manpower
6. Added value
7. Sender, Dominion (Ownership) 8. Alienation
9. Extortion
10. Kingdom

These are the basic concepts and words used by Marx and Engels in their analysis of capitalist industrial societies in the text Capital Investment. It is explained how sects are finally formed in the evolution of these. Due to the formation of sects, it was felt that class struggle was necessary. For that, they gathered the contradictions in many fields and the unity between the contradictions to support their argument. emphasized the need for class struggle. Lenin described the unity in contradiction and the universality of contradiction as:-

1. +, -, Differential, Integral in Mathematics
2. Action in mechanics, reaction
3. Positive electricity, negative electricity in physics
4. Combination, Fission of Molecules in Chemistry
5. Class Struggle in Sociology

Two contradictions are mentioned in the first four points above. It is said that in sociology there is only one aspect which is class struggle instead of two aspects. Mao also mentioned it as it is but left out the second point.

It is agreed that there is unity and conflict in conflict. According to that, in sociology there are two aspects namely unity between classes and struggle between classes. There should be both class struggle and unity of classes. The second point is not left just like that. Marxists define that all history is the history of class struggles. They were not concerned about unity among communities. History exists only if there is a class struggle. That is, wars and conflicts are history. The coexistence of human society is not history. Thus they prioritized class struggles for co-existence and left the ultimate goal of co-existence and its priority. Some agreements are reached when workers, industrialists, after a class struggle. According to those agreements, the workers work together with the industrialists. Government employees and teachers also mobilize for their demands. They go on Strikes. Agreements are made. Both parties will accept those agreements and work together. It is an ongoing union between employer, workers and employees. Coexistence of all. They put forward some more demands and movements for coexistence.

Therefore both unity and conflict exist in all spheres. Class struggle is not alone in the social sphere. If it is said so, then the fundamental formula that there are two opposites in one object becomes void.

Marxism could not apply its formulation to the social spheres itself. Neither in historical materialism nor in the struggles of the working class, apart from the class struggle, the discussion of unity between classes, their history, their evolution and their importance is not recognized. Has Ranganayakamma read such fundamentals, noticed, discussed ? No.

From Marx and Engel to Mao, continued to apply the philosophical discussion about 'Thing in Itself', 'Thing for itself' to the class. Mao vehemently argued that there is only class in itself, class for itself and no class for others. Jean Paul Satre also said that there is being in itself and being for oneself but not being for others. Engels discusses this discussion of the possibility of an object becoming a Thing for Us. But he never said that there will be a class for others. Buddha emphasized altruism. People like Kalidasa opined that the human body is for serving others and the body is for fulfilling of dharma. Charity should be done. But he said that it is possible only when this body is a tool. Altruism is supreme among human values, culture and human relations. This philanthropic practice, emphasized from the Buddha to today, if translated into philosophical terms,

Marxism - Socialism

becomes Class for Others. Class for Others is a noble practice of philanthropy and humanitarian culture. Marx, Engels, Lenin, Mao were not born in the working class. Did not grow as working class. Mark, Lenin and Mao belonged to the petty bourgeoisie. Engels himself was an industrialist with a textile mill. With the profits from the textile mill, Marx edited Capital and other books and published them under his editorship. By all means he extended co-operation by sheltering Birla Gandhi, the owner of a cloth mill in India.

Due to the belief of Class for Others in Marx and Engels, because of humane values of helping others, culture and practice of philanthropy, they stood on the side of the working class which was not theirs and worked hard for them. This is not possible without class for others and philanthropy.

Lenin's formula that if someone works with working class consciousness, they can become working class, which becomes possible through the practice of class for others and philanthropy. Otherwise, there is no chance for anyone else to circulate as a working class except the workers. Did Ranganayakamma discuss class in itself, class for self, class for others? Did she know there was such a thing? No... Not known.

It was discovered by the time of Marx and Engels that there are electrons and protons in an object. With its support it is theorized that there will be both unity and conflict in the social sphere. But in 1937, it was discovered that there is a third element called neutron in addition to electron and proton. It was learned that there are many other elements besides the neutron. When taken from science and applied to social sciences and fields, Marxism should support that there are three elements in the social field namely unity, conflict, neutrality, struggle between classes, unity between classes and neutrality between classes. Also Einstein's discovery of the speed of light and the theory of relativity should be applied in social sciences and social fields. It follows science and backs up truths. But neither in Marxist political economics nor in social sciences did they add these truths and create new concepts and theories in accordance with the newly discovered truths. They were not enriched. The above two elements will be enriched and will be like what is given below:-

1. $+, - =$ in mathematics

2. In mechanics action, reaction, action beyond reaction
3. Physics Positive, Negative, Neutral, Electron, Proton, Neutron
4. Combination, fission, status co, stability of molecules in chemistry
5. Unity, conflict, neutrality, unity between classes, struggle between classes, neutrality between classes in sociology.

Thus many examples can be given that two elements are also three elements in motion, in contrast, in particular, in universal.

1. Past	Present	Future
2. Past Tense in Language	Present Tense	Future Tense
3. Solid state	Liquid State	Airy state, invisible state period
4. Place	Time	Existence, consciousness
5. I	You	He
6. First Person	Second Person	Third Person
7. Birth	Death	Life
8. Action	Reaction	Inertia, Stability
9. Best	Medium	Low
10. Wrong	Yes	Relativity
11. Illusion	Imagination	Reality
12. Mindy	Bodily	Karma
13. Governing Body		Oppressed class Middle Class
14. Inevitability	Coincidence	Passion, Interest
15. Particular	All particulars	Universal
16. In himself	For himself	Himself for others

It can be observed that there are three elements in many sciences and fields. It has been said that Marxism is made up of the scientific aspects of the natural sciences and social sciences. Science is constantly evolving. New practices, experiences and theories are

Marxism - Socialism

constantly emerging in social sciences. The development of science is causing changes in production relations and human relations. Many changes in strategy and tactics were inevitable. For example, after the invention of aircraft and bombs, the forts and their structures became useless. Therefore, the strategy, tactics, programs and military structure of the war changed. Also every innovation is contributing to changes in the social sector in many aspects. In Marxism, this science is updated only when it grows and incorporates the effects and consequences of innovations into the social sciences. Otherwise, the views and strategic moves that have stopped in those olden times of science will continue.

Nothing is permanent. Everything is impermanent, everything is subject to change. The movements of self, self for self and self for others change in relation to each other. In Marxism, it is thought that there is a thing in itself, a thing for itself. Although Engels said that a thing can be changed into a thing for itself, Mao emphasized that there is only class in itself, class for itself and no class for others. Buddhism and humanism emphasize mutual beneficence and altruism. Benevolence means class for others; mutual benefit means mutual aid and cooperation between groups and ranks. Marx, Engels, Lenin, Mao and others ignored the human values, culture and perspective of mutual benefit and altruism. They were concerned with Unity between opposites, conflict is evolutionary, qualitative change, negation only. They have applied it to the society mechanically.

According to the principle of the unity of opposites, if there were no slaves, there would be no slave owners. So if it exists, that exists. Pratitya Samutpada discusses that if it perishes, that perishes. Marxism also deals with negation. There is no Hitlerism without Marxism and Leninism. Without the socialism of Marxism, there is no National Socialism of Hitler. Because it exists, the other exists. Working class socialist governments named Marxist Marxism and other factions came into leadership in the name of working-class leadership. The Dictatorship continued. Finally, the state socialism was also abandoned and the private capitalist industrial system was brought forward. As if the earthis round, they turned back to private capitalism and mixed economy. But, in the political field, the multi-party system was suppressed and the dictatorship continued. Consequently, the leadership of the working-class party lost its basic spirit and became the leadership of the respective leaders. However, still based on them, they are trying to come to power in their name. Engels finally said a word. What we have written in our whole life, in short, we have only said that we should uncover the motion patterns in the respective object, society and problem. Apart from that, they did not ask to apply the principles formulated by them and say that such motions exist.

By saying that anyone can become the working class and the leadership of the working class with this consciousness, they came to power and became dictators. While these developments took place in Buddhism, Shaivism and Vaishnavism centuries later, Marxism and Socialism could not continue beyond a few decades. Selfishness dominated and they and their relatives evolved into industrialists. The ambition to build an ideal world socialism with the sacrifices of billions of people collapsed within a few decades after coming to power. Even though the non-working-class people disguise themselves as the working class and seize power and call it Marxism, in practice they become bourgeois and industrialists, and in practice Marxism and socialism are collapsing. The question "Is it necessary for millions of people to make sacrifices and martyrdom with movements and armed struggles for such an evolution?" spread among the people.

Ambedkarism - Socialism

Babasaheb Ambedkar is well known among the builders of socialism in the world. World revolutionary, human rights movement leader, well-known economist, sociologist who paved the way to achieve social justice, social change, freedom equality, fraternity, classless, casteless, genderless, socialism in a democratic system. In world history, Ambedkar's practical theories of socialism, Ambedkarism are an integral part. Ambedkar's contribution to the world socialist theories, systems and forms of struggle is great.

Ambedkar lived in a time when the theories of Marx, Engels, Lenin, Stalin, Mao, Freud, Tolstoy were becoming a new physical force. The period between the birth and death (1891-1956) was the greatest historical period in the history of the world. This period gave birth to many theories, revolutions, wars and new inventions. Ambedkarism is one of them. Ambedkarism is a specific form of socialism in Indian historical social developments.

Socialism has spread throughout the world in different forms, theories and practice in different countries. It is the diversity in the particularities of the place and country that gave birth to these different forms and ideologies. From the Buddha's time, the Buddha proposed and practiced socialism as the Buddham Saranam Gachami, Dhammam Saranam Gachami and Sangham Saran Gachami Buddha's philosophy is 'Pratitya Samutpada'.

Revolution, love, compassion, wisdom, wisdom, virtue, Ashtanga way personality development, social "Bahujana Hitaya, Bahujana Sukhaya" were proposed and practiced by Buddha. From two and a half years, the Buddhist and social socialist revolution continues even today.

Like Spartacus and Moses, Babasaheb Ambedkar rose from the poor for the poor. Abraham Lincoln, Stalin, Mao etc. who grew up from poverty were in power for a long time. So that they would have a chance to put what they thought into practice and check the results. Ambedkar was not like that. In this regard, Marx, Lenin, Gramsci and Ambedkar have similarities.

Lenin and Ambedkar Cheguvera have close similarities in some respects. They have great interest in acquiring knowledge. Extensive study was their favorite task. They have been in power for a short time. They influenced all sectors of their country.

The argument that Ambedkarism and socialism are not the same is not correct. There are two types of them. One says Ambedkarism is higher than socialism. Hence they say that both are not one. Another says that there is no comparison between Ambedkarism and socialism and say that Ambedkarism is untouchable.

Both sides need to understand that nothing comes from a vacuum. By understanding how far history has gone, it is possible to predict how to move forward. Therefore, both capitalist democracy and Marxism were indispensable in the growth of Ambedkarism.

Mao was three years younger than Ambedkar. Both were born in backward, agrarian countries with large populations and both were born in Asia. Mao lived until 1976. Ambedkar died in 1956. Thus there is a historical limit of 1956 for Ambedkar in the ideas of socialism.

While the Soviet model of state socialism became a revisionism, Mao got an opportunity to think new ideas in the political fields. While studying Ambedkarism as another model of socialism, there are some other points to be considered.

For example - if Lincoln, Lenin, Stalin, Mao were the heads of state, Ambedkar was a minister who did not keep his word in any cabinet he was in. He was at a historical stage where he had to face the social (caste) oppression that no one else had faced, and his untouchability in addition and find solutions.

Ambedkarism - Socialism

Even though Ambedkar died in 1956, there are few things that he foresaw things better than Mao. For example - Ambedkar started the Great Cultural Revolution in 1956 by converting millions to Buddhism. Ten years later Mao started the Cultural Revolution in China. To be precise, Ambedkar recognized the need for a cultural revolution 40 years before Mao. Fore seeing revisionism, social imperialism 30 years before, it was Ambedkar who proposed new solutions to the flaws in the socialist models of Russia and China (Whether Mao welcomed or protested when Ambedkar embraced Buddhism along with millions of others is not known)

What is Ambedkarism? Ambedkarism, in Marxist terms, is the model of socialism that Marxists call, liberty, equality, fraternity, individual freedom, one person, one value, justifiable development, achieved by persuasion of the majority, social democracy, multi-party system, abolition of caste, cultural revolutions by the synthesis or coordination of development. A comprehensive study of Ambedkar will make this clear.

Ambedkar had as much aversion on small scale production as Lenin. Lenin advocated that small-scale production reproduces the Individual Capitalist Ownership. Ambedkar asserted that small-scale production will result in the dominance of the upper caste, will promote caste and caste-based works, and inhumanity towards oppressed castes.

Ambedkar said that the caste-based rural republics (self-sufficient rural system) could not effectively repel foreign attacks, that there should be centralized industries, that the basic industries should remain in government ownership, and that minorities should have complete security. He wanted to nationalize insurance companies. "Kalipatnam Rama Rao wrote a non-fiction story called 'Kutra'. He says that there is a conspiracy of investors behind the demand to put infrastructure- industries under government ownership. Many people read it and thought it must be true. They did not know that it was actually not a conspiracy but that Ambedkar had fought a lot of ideological struggles for it and it was a Soviet model. Even those who oppose privatization today will realize that it is not a conspiracy. If it is a conspiracy then why oppose privatization today?

In 1918, Ambedkar, wrote in his theoretical book, called for the nationalization of land, the recognition of agriculture as an industry, the abolition of small plots, the payment of compensation for land in the form of debentures, etc. and interest on them, to show them other occupations, collective farming and reduce population pressure on farming. Ambedkar's foresight can be understood if we realize that collective farming was not shaped by then in the Soviet Union.

Ambedkar also hoped that the nationalization of land and infrastructure industries and the establishment of heavy industries in the public sector would help solve the caste problem.

But infrastructural, national and heavy industries have transformed the local upper castes into national level upper castes. A strong center and political democracy helped to unite the regional elites at the national level in all spheres of ethnic life. If Ambedkar had lived a little longer, he would have noticed this and reconsidered.

The Soviet system and the Commune system in China inspired the formation of Zilla Parishads, Panchayats and Mandals in our country. The commune model is the same as if all the government departments work under their control along with the existing departments. If the land is nationalized then this is almost a complete commune model.

Before examining Ambedkar's model of socialism, some historical facts need to be considered. The Marx left the unity in contradictions between the oppressed and the ruling class. In other words, unity in contradiction - not two conflicts but one conflict. Mao worked hard to build unity with the ruling classes. What Mao did was right, and what Ambedkar did was seen as wrong by some, but it was nothing but the perspective of the elites. Ambedkar discussed the struggle for unity with the ruling classes more comprehensively than Mao at all levels. Mao's emphasis was primarily on a unified event in the fields of political and economic struggle. Ambedkar extended it in all spheres. Ambedkar's writing of the Constitution of India was a supreme form of unity of the oppressed with the ruling class.

If Ambedkar had survived till 1976 like Mao, what would have been the history of the world? Then how would Ambedkar have studied the world history? These are the questions that serve to raise Ambedkarism. After Ambedkar's death, Ambedkarism lacked high-level leadership. Hence the above questions are being asked.

Ambedkarism - Socialism

Stalin failed to study the Indian national movement properly. He seems to be relying on second-hand information from the communist elite boys. If it was observed directly, the effect would have been different when the joint Communist Party was banned because it was working with the Congress for such a long time without building any unity event with forces like Ambedkar and Komuram Bhim. Dalit forces and revolutionary forces would have grown into a strong force and Dalit leadership would have developed greatly. B.C. Reservations would have been achieved by 1940, if not since the Poona Pact of 1932.

The fear of insecurity brought by the world wars, the principles of party formation created by Lenin, and the socialist model shown by Marxism combined to make Stalin undemocratic. Even the Soviet people might want to put up with it because of that. Ambedkar condemned Stalin's undemocracy. Hence Ambedkar could not show the same interest in Stalin as he did show in Mao.

But Ambedkar adopted the educational system introduced by Stalin (during), planned development with social justice, development of socialist culture, etc. Some items he developed himself. Until recently, Marxist socialism proposed in India lacked a Dalit perspective and a feminist perspective. Assessing how they would have behaved if they had existed is very useful for today's practice. If Ambedkar had lived till 1976 or in 1950 or 1967 (when the opposition came to power in half of the states, if he had been the Prime Minister of India, there would have been many changes in China-India relations. Mao and Ambedkar would have changed in the order of mutual understanding, and thus there would have been significant changes in various areas of democracy in China and in our country. The views of Mao and Ambedkar are close about socialist democracy. It can be said that Ambedkar did not have Gorbachev's illusions about western democracy.

Ambedkar disagreed with Abraham Lincoln's definition of democracy. In Lincoln's view, democracy means "of the people, by the people, for the people". In Ambedkar's view, democracy means higher goals. In his view, democracy means bringing about fundamental changes in the social and economic life of the people, overcoming differences without bloodshed and achieving them with the consent of the people. For that, theoretically, academically, culturally and socially it is needed to develop the people continuously. In short, to achieve socialism through cultural, social, economic, political and peaceful revolutions through mutual cooperation, freedom, equality and brotherhood by providing facilities and knowledge to the people.

For some Marxists and Leninists, it is common to argue that democracy means elections. Ambedkar proposed Social Democracy. In Babasaheb's view, democracy means living together. The origin of democracy is to be found in the social relations of the people who make up the society. Ambedkar's aim was to bring the philosophical concept of one person and only one value, one vote into practice in all spheres. There is no theory beyond this in the world.

A comparative study of the theories of Mao and Ambedkar teaches us one thing. Before moving to socialism, Mao proposed a "new democratic revolutionary phase" in the agrarian country of China. Mao's proposal that the new democratic revolution would be led by the working class, including the peasantry, would lead to a transition to socialism without the need for another bloody revolution. The Naxalites adopted this as applicable to our country with minor modifications.

A new democratic revolution is an accelerating capitalist revolution under the leadership of the working class. Converting agricultural plots into collective plots, setting up basic industries in the government sector, accelerating capitalist development, reducing population pressure on agriculture and moving them to new occupations, increasing crop yields, subsidizing essential sectors, in a nut shell is an economic program. Interestingly, Ambedkar as a renowned economist mentioned these as urgent tasks as early as 1919. Many people do not know that Ambedkar's contribution to world economics was immense. Hence Kabul Ambedkar Universal University on 17th and 18th January 1992 conducted an UGC seminar on 20 topics about Ambedker's Philo-sophy and brought many things to light. Most of the topics discussed here are the same.

In Ambedkar's writings and practices (1915 to 1956) a new democratic revolution tailored to India's specific conditions was clearly shaped. Ambedkar's gift of unity with the ruling class was to give constitutional representation to the new democratic revolution and socialism, as Mao and the Naxalites said, and enshrined them in

Ambedkarism - Socialism

the directive principles as the objectives of the constitution. Combining Ambedkar's writings with the constitutions of the Soviets and Communes, and the extent to which they were reflected in his constitution, it can be clearly understood.

By constitutionalizing a subject, a goal, it gains moral support as a value to be practiced. For example - if there is no Minimum Wages Act, Leave Act then we want to make them. We want the laws to be implemented once they become laws. That is, legitimacy is an achievement in the realm of thought. Implementation is the achievement of practicing it.

It is naïve to say that if an officer does not grant leave then the leave law is inoperative. The real task will be to pressurize by the union whether to grant leave while recognizing the Act and to make the grant of leave more liberal. When the goals of the new democratic revolution said by the Naxalites have constitutional support, the real task is to mobilize the people in the political, social and economic fields in order to speed them up. These achievements of Ambedkar make it clear that the Naxalite outlook is 70 years behind. Many articles in the constitution testify to the continuing constitutional commitment to the new democratic revolution and socialism.

According to Ambedkar, the Constitution of India aimed at radically changing the socio-economic structure. If the constitution written by Ambedkar is converted to socialist terms, none of Indian Communist Manifestos can be better than that. If it is questioned whether that is in force or then it should be questioned whether these are in force. Ambedkar also declared that he would not hesitate to burn the constitution which he had written with such hopes if those goals were not achieved within the stipulated time. Can communists and naxalites dare say the same on communist manifesto on their documents?

Ambedkar wanted political reservation for 10 years. It means that he believed that in 10 years people should develop socially, economically, ideologically and politically so fast. Ambedkar was so concerned on the pace of social change.

There are close similarities between the views of Soviet leader Rosa Luxemburg, Italian Communist Party leader Granci and other socialists who did not join the communist camp and Ambedkar's ideas.

It is because of the different geographical conditions in culture, social structure, political structure, consciousness and economic level that some countries came into existence as separate countries. Gramsci said that every country has a special way to achieve socialism and the first task of the communists of the respective countries is to explore this way. Lenin in Russia, Granci in Italy and MaoYi in China performed this duty. Our communists and naxalites did not seek their own way but copied someone else. It is heartening to recognize this need now. Now they are bringing out not only Lenin and Mao but all kinds of ideas of the communist school of the world. As a part of it, Ambedkarism, Gramsci and feminism were started to be compared and accepted. Granci died in 1937.

Unable to have come to power themselves, the proposed theory of peaceful transition may have led to revisionism and social imperialism. But Gramsci discovered the analysis of the correct historical forces involved thirty years earlier.

Paris Commune, Soviet Revolution, World Revolutions, Development of Democratic Powers Social Consequences One Person One Value Principle, More History, Culture Consequences Ruling Classes, Ruling Castes, Ruling Sexes, Ruling Races, Ruling Nations, With Oppressed Classes, are constantly facing historic compromise with Oppressed Castes, Oppressed Sexes, Oppressed Communities, Oppressed countries. Thus, the successes achieved by the popular movements get constitutional recognition and bring changes in the culture in social, political, economic, legal and administrative fields. Socialists, Gramsci, Ambedkar, Lenin, Mao and other historical forces have taken up a new perspective, strategy, moves and programs to give theoretical support to this historical development that has been going on since the period of change.

After the perestroika developments, the whole world is realizing that the Russian revolution of 1917 was not a socialist revolution, but a national democratic revolution. Most Marxist-Leninists agree that socialist revolutions are not possible except democratic revolutions in backward countries. National democratic revolutions were successful in different ways in Russia, China and India.

Ambedkarism - Socialism

Gramsci felt that the concept of 'dictatorship of the proletariat' was wrong. Grancy emphasized that enforcement was by popular consent. Ambedkar said exactly this. Grancy's concept of civil society and Ambedkar's concept of social democracy are closely related.

"Evolution" is another key point in Gramsci's concept. This was adopted by the Communist Party of Italy as "fundamental reforms". Gramsci developed a view of taking power by changing the constitution rather than by overthrowing it. Ambedkar practiced and showed it. He developed it further. Ambedkar strove to constitutionalize the new democratic socialist goals by enshrining them in the Directive Principles.

Ambedkar hoped to achieve the same value in socio-economic fields through political democracy of one person one value, one vote. He defined capitalism as the dictatorship of the private owner.

On 26 January 1950, Ambedkar said about the new constitution " We would have equality in the political sphere. There is inequality in socio-economic life". In politics we are going to recognize the principle of one man one vote, one value. Because of our socioeconomic structure we are going to continue to deny a man a value principle in our social and economic life. How long will we deny these contradictions in life? If we want to refuse for a long time it will only be possible by putting our political democracy at risk. We must eliminate this contradiction as soon as possible. If that is not done, those who are oppressed by inequality will demolish the structure of political democracy that this Constituent Assembly has so painstakingly built.

Ambedkar's ambition to achieve social democracy and economic democracy through political democracy did not materialize.

Political democracy for its own political benefits, reinforcing the old social (caste) structure of inequality. There is no shortage of forces striving to achieve social and economic democracy in life through political democracy. It is because of them that public life has developed to this extent. communists and Naxalites also believe that socio-economic democracy can be achieved in life only through the political democracy of the oppressed class and building movements.

There-fore, there is unity in outlook and practice between Marxism, Socialism and Ambedkarism.

At the same time Ambedkar made some changes to the understanding of world socialism. He did not accept the Marxist formulation that the state was merely an instrument of oppression. The ultimate goal of socialism is to increase the nature of welfare within the state through the state. Ambedkar was the one who constantly worked for it. Buddhism first proposed the transformation of the state into a welfare nature. Emperor Ashoka practiced it and demonstrated it. Two and a half thousand years later, Marx and Engels said in the discussion of Communism and Socialism that they had newly discovered that the state could be converted into a welfare state.

Marxism says that the state arises and continues through the right to property. Ambedkar elevated it further. Ambedkar asserted that the possession of knowledge, knowledge as a right and the refusal to give knowledge the exploitation and oppression of the state continued through, and the Brahminism has done the same for hundreds of years. In other words, Ambedkar made it clear that the state's oppression stems from knowledge being a private property right.

Marxists used the theory of inevitability for socialism to overthrow the exploitative forces in existence through the use of force, saying that revolution was inevitable(Theory of Karma).

Ambedkar fundamentally disagreed with both of these. Ambedkar practiced and showed that interest, perseverance and knowledge are important for people to make revolutions, and if it is there, there is a way to solve social conflicts by achieving the consent of the people without much use of force by speeding up the ideological revolution. Thus, Ambedkar made many fundamental contributions to the thought and practice of socialism in the world. Important among them are:-

1. To prove that it is possible to work for the development of social democracy with social justice by giving constitutional representation for the goals of socialism in the constitutional machinery with the support of political democracy, .

2. To shed the constitutional machinery of its repressive nature and make a trans-formative effort towards a welfare state.

Ambedkarism - Socialism

3. Ambedkar's discussion of Brahmanism confirms that alienation, oppression, and the state arise not only from individual property, but also from the denial of property, knowledge, control, and knowledge.

4. He practiced and showed that socialism can be achieved by other means without working under the dictator-ship of the working class.

5. In an agricultural country, Ambedkar achieved another thing which was not achieved by either Mao in China, communists or Naxalites in our country. By seeking participation in education, employment opportunities and industrial develop-ment through reservations, the way to reduce population pressure on the land was laid. In Marxist terms, the conflict between the feudal system and the rest of the masses is not resolved as a class conflict and transferred sections of the subject of people to the more developed relations of production, capitalist and professional occupations. As a result, solving the class conflict and social conflict by splitting the two sides and fighting has ended and was limited to solving it as a program to eradicate the remnants.

6. "Earth for tillage" promises people a life that is back-ward from the capitalist society and time. Thus, in the name of revolutionary victory, it gives the people the back-wardness of living constantly behind the capitalist profiteers. In this practice, everything in capitalist development is left to the whims of the ruling classes and ruling castes. It is the rights achieved through reservation that allow participation in this.

According to Ambedkar, the objective of the Indian Constitution was to bring about a complete change in the socio-economic structure of India. Ambedkar challenged that if the guiding principles of these constitutional directives are not socialist in essence, then I have failed to understand what socialism is. Ambedkarism has added many fundamental things and achievements in the socialism that Marxism says and in the practice of the whole idea of socialism. Thus Ambedkarism became an integral part of world socialism. Ambedkar's contribution to socialism

B.S Ramulu

Dr. BR Ambedkar as an economist
Topics discussed in this

1. Ambedkar as Indian Social Economist
2. Ambedkar as Indian Political Economist
3. Ambedkar as Indian Social Welfare Economist
4. Ambedkar as a planned economist
5. Indian interests as an international economist at the center
6. Ambedkar as an Indian monetary (financial) economist
7. Ambedkar as Economist of Indian Urbanization
8. Ambedkar as Indian Social Development Scientist
9. As an economist who changed the Indian social structure
10. Ambedkar as an economist concerned with the relation of religion, caste and ideology to economics.
11. As a social worker who discussed semiology as a social science
12. Ambedkar as Buddhist Economist

Ambedkar's contribution towards social issues, towards caste, towards Hinduism, and towards constitution architecture is most popular. Dr. B.R. Ambedkar's contribution to economics has not been much scrutinized. People know less about Ambedkar as an economist. Being an economist, Ambedkar became a philosopher of caste abolition who clearly observed the role caste plays in economics. Abolition of caste, adoption of Buddhism, democratic administration etc. also describes Ambedkar's work as an economist. Ambedkar wrote extensively about the rupee problem, about exports and imports, about nationalization of lands, about nationalization of insurance companies and heavy industries, about achieving social equality, political equality, economic equality in a multi-party system. Ambedkar can be understood as an economist when all these are codified.

Dr. B.R. Ambedkar studied economics as a student. He wrote his first research paper on economics in 1913 at the age of 24. Thesis on 'Administration of East India Company - Financial Policy' M.A. submitted for degree. This is the first article written by Ambedkar. A

Ambedkarism - Socialism

second book was written in 1924 entitled Evolution of the State Economy in British India – A Study of State Decentralization in the Imperial Economy. A book on the history of Indian currency banking - The Rupee Problem - was also published. He wrote a review on the Report of the Commission for the Study of Taxation, Currency Exchange, 1926.

Barter During the visit of India between 1924-25 to India's Social Insurance Royal Commission on Indian Currency, and FinancialAffairs to examine the economy and suggest changes in Indian currency policyof Ambedkar's.

He examined Barter System, Indian Social Insurance, Indian Currency, Financial affairs of Royal Commission and to suggest changes in Indian currency policy during the visit of India between 1924-25, Dr Ambedkar's questionnaire, evidence and statements were recorded and submitted. For gaining MA, during the year 1913-15 he made a research on the topics like the Ancient Indian trade, India's trade relations in the Middle East, India's trade relations in the Middle Ages, British rule. Ambedkar made more than a thousand pages of research and conclusions about this 'Arthashastra'. These Ambedkar's writings and speeches were compiled in volumes 6 and 12.

Ambedkar did much research on economics as a student before becoming a social activist. He took PhD in Economics. However, in the process of working as a social activist, Ambedkar noticed that economics is not independent of itself, and the social system, government policies, administration, religion, caste, ideology, have a nature to rule economics, but all the social sciences are broken up and examined for convenience, and by observing them that are all interdependent in society, Ambedkar took care of all of them. He further went on to research and analyze.

1. Ambedkar as an Indian Social Economist

Therefore on examination of Ambedkar's other writings, the entire social practice he can be classified as a social economist in economics. Moving from economics to philosophy, to sociology, Ambedkar took the caste system, the varna system and the Hindu religious system seriously. Thus he evolved into a social philosopher. All this is part of the effort to address the obstacles to the development of Indian society as a whole. He condemned the theories of Karma, which for centuries restricted the majority of people to certain tasks and prevents the development of productive forces and intelligence and destroyed the theories of,reincarnation , caste system and varna system. He went on to declare that all these are an obstacle for India to grow as a developed country in the world, making human resources useless and pushing them into poverty. Thus, so many things were included within the scope of social economics and enriched it. Some do not think of it as such and discuss it as an ideological debate and leave Ambedkar's socio-economic goals behind. It was inevitable for Ambedkar, as an economist and a sociologist, to be aware of all this.

2. Ambedkar as Indian Political Economist

As an economist Ambedkar adopted the best of earlier economics. He developed economics in his own sense. Some have examined economics in terms of capital, commodities, profits, labor power, surplus value, state, etc. Ricardo, Marx, Engels examined society and social system through capital, commodities, profits, labor power, surplus value, state etc. They went on to say that the economy determines the social system. Others have examined the ruling classes and the measures taken by the government for their welfare as a field of economics.

He made it clear how those who are under the control of government, society, caste, class, agricultural parties, industrial ownership etc. get economic and social benefits and rule others. Hence Ambedkar as an economist analyzed all the problems of India, all the aspects with Indian specific interests. Hindu Brahminism rooted in superstitions, caste system theories and share in state power were taken seriously. Ambedkar felt that reservations are also a part of economics.

Ambedkar deeply examined the relationship between politics, administration, economics and the development of people's lives. In the book of ancient trade of India, he examined how wars, dominance over those areas, means of transportation of goods, etc., have brought many changes in the societies, religions, people's lives in India. Marx, Engels, European and American economists examined the social sciences and economics according to the political social power center of Europe and America. In other words, they discussed the social

Ambedkarism - Socialism

sciences and development of Asian countries as a result of alienating, collecting and suppressing policies. Ambedkar, in contrast to this, observed India as the center and Asian countries as an example, and explained how the European countries exploited and suppressed them. Thus Ambedkar's Arthasastra has a fundamental difference from western.Arthasastra .

Ambedkar as a political economist closely examined the history of India, production systems, castes, Muslim invasions, European migrations and their exploitation. The Roman emperors brandished their swords in both the eastern and western directions. Ambedkar noted that the results were different, that in the East "they conquered only to punish" and in the West they wanted to Romanize their rulers. Thus, starting from the ancient trade relations to the British period, the Indian trade economy was examined from the Indian sphere.

Ambedkar investigated the agricultural system, labour-intensive industries, trade and their management in ancient India. He discussed the effect of the transport, water ways and road beds in their role of commerce

He explained how money entered India. It is mentioned in the Buddhist literature recorded that the method of barter, which was in place since ancient times, and the method of estimating by calculating the measurements of rice, by counting the cows, gradually came into use of metal. According to Gautama, there are six types of interest on loans.

As an example, it is explained that there has been traffic in the northern part of the Indian Ocean since the early days of history. It is observed that the arrival of Babylonia was a major turning point in ancient Indian trade activities. Historically ascertained how India maintained trade with Greek, Roman, Babylonian and Mesopotamian civilizations. The advent of Islam had a profound effect on the economic, political, and commercial expansion of Western Europe. Encouraged by the economic powers of the time, the new converts to Mohammedanism (in 668–675 AD) besieged Constantinople. Whoever dominated Constantinople ruled the economies and trades of Asia and Europe. Thus the role played by political social developments in economics is historically assessed.

It is well explained how economically advanced India was during the British rule. India contributed a lot to the prosperity of England. Or Ambedkar says it is correct to say that India was made to contribute towards the prosperity of England. It is based on British records that the British colonialists systematically destroyed India's trade and caste industry. Ambedkar's assessment of the extent to which India was destroyed to make it a market for European industrial products is comprehensive. By the manner in which all political and social developments are explained as part of Arthasastra brought a distinctiveness to Ambedkar's approach to economic analysis.

3. Ambedkar as Indian Social Welfare Economist

Ambedkar examined Arthasastra with the focus of social development, social justice, social change, equality and freedom. How should the government be? How are the social classes? What should be the distribution system for social justice? How should the powers be and in whose hands? etc. Ambedkar took economics seriously. Ambedkar's economics can therefore be defined as social welfare economics.

Social welfare is the basic theme of Ambedkar's economics. Most of the modern economists have written economics focusing on Western countries, their development, interests, their needs, their resources and way of life. Many of them. It was considered sufficient to apply to India as is and put into practice. Dr. B.R. Ambedkar, on the other hand, took India as the center and developed Indian economics as social welfare economics, taking into account domestic interests, resources, ways of life, needs, culture, caste discrimination and inequality.

Like the path to heaven, the path of social reform is a difficult and full of thorns. A monster named 'caste' stands in the way. Dr. B Ambedkar clarified that political reforms and economic reforms will not come until this devil is killed. This statement makes it clear that Ambedkar was very much aware of the limitations of Arthasastra.

4. Ambedkar as Indian Planned Economist

Ambedkar was also an economist who proposed planned development. Many suggestions were made about the economic development to be done in the pre-independence period during the British rule in the colonies. He also made many suggestions to the Nizam about the Nizam's kingdom. All these are yet to be included in

Ambedkarism - Socialism

Ambedkar's supplementary works. It may not be possible to include all his life time work ever. Hence it becomes necessary to codify the sentiments of those days by social practice.

Ambedkar expressed a clear vision of planned development like Russia after independence. Nehru's vision was the same. Nehru's prominence as Prime Minister increased hundreds of times and many things were popularized in Nehru's name. There was a debate in the country about Nehru's economic policy and Gandhi's economic policy. Was even incorporated into textbooks. Rammanohar Lohia, Mao and Gandhi called for decentralization of power and industrialization as rural development is important. Ambedkar strongly opposed this. Ambedkar felt that the old modes of production, the villages, would reproduce the caste system and caste discrimination, again and again.

Just as the Congress abandoned Gandhi's policies after independence, they abandoned Ambedkar too. There is a need to seperately discuss Ambedkar's economic policy, who studied thousands of texts and made significant contributions in economics.

Since the Congress party was in the government, even the insignificant words of their leaders were widely propagated as economic theories. There are very few people who thought like Ambedkar after him. Still, it is necessary to codify Ambedkar's views as Gandhi, Nehru, and Velibucha's views were codified in those cases as their economic theories. People subjected to planned oppression of social justice and oppressed should be developed through providing special opportunities and Ambedkar considered reservation as a means to develop through.

Ambedkar was one of those who felt the importance of planning commission and five year plans for planned development. He felt that it is very necessary to give subsidies when necessary as incentives for the products and services needed by the society. Theory of reservation and theory of subsidy both belong to the same category. He said that employment of human resources, development of irrigation facilities, power generation, development of infrastructural heavy industries and development of large water projects are essential for the Indian economy. Ambedkar had some clear views on how the taxation system should be.

Ambedkar thought that banks and insurance companies should be nationalized and large industries should be owned by the government. Ambedkar in his student days gave good formulations on the land problem in India that land should be nationalized and dividends should be given to the land owners so that land transfer can be done peacefully.

Adivasis and Dalits, who were backward, have worked hard to achieve modern development through reservations. Thus, the pressure of people on agriculture is reduced and the burden of people on agriculture is reduced. Ambedkar made it clear that as the British suppressed the professions in India as sellers of their industrial goods through high taxes and otherwise, all those who lost their professions turned to agriculture, thus increasing the human pressure on agriculture as never before.

By fighting for a share in modern development Ambedkar was able to greatly reduce the pressure on agriculture and land caused by the British. But some Communists and Naxalites did not study the pressure of the people on the land due to the policies of the British, but they increased the pressure on the land by saying that the "land belongs to its plowmen" which made the landlords to run for the modern development and thus, the people who need to get the modern development were pushed into the land.

Thus, the Communists and Naxalites continued their efforts in the interests of the ruling classes in India to bring them to modern development. Looking at it from this point of view, it is clear that the social consequences of reservation have to be examined from many angles.

5. Ambedkar as an International Economist with Indian interests as the central focus.

Ambedkar extensively studied the history of ancient world trade. These were amply recorded in the report given to the Simon Commission. It has been confirmed in many ways that the role played by India in world history is great and India's contribution to world civilizations and culture is crucial. He examined the history, trade, religion, invasion, wars and civilizations and suggested the way to have an international Indian historical and economic perspective.

Ambedkarism - Socialism

However, after independence, the castes and communities who joined the Congress government and the employment sectors practiced the international Indian historical economic perspective as the offspring of those castes and others as the offspring of Western socio-economic theories. Thus the country gradually evolved to accept their superiority philosophically , in historiography, in economic historiography as vassalage to foreign countries, and in order to eventually become dependent country after the GATT and globalization agreements.

Ambedkar's writings make it clear that this predicament would not have arisen if Arthasastra was adopted with international perspective.

6. Ambedkar as an Indian monetary (financial) economist

Ambedkar analyzed how the circulation of coins took place after money replaced barter in India over the centuries. He discussed what standards were taken by the kings in printing gold, silver and copper coins. Ambedkar brought before us the principles followed by the Muslim kings and British rulers in coinage and values and the effects they had on trade and people's lives.

British monetary policies provide a rich overview of how India determined the value of the rupee in British economic relations. Due to many such observations, the value of dollar, pound and rupee continued to be equal to each other until 1947. The rupee has now devalued to ___ rupees to the dollar and ___ rupees to the pound. This predicament would not have happened if the value of the rupee had been assessed as the center of Indian interests after independence in the light spread by Ambedkar.

7. Ambedkar as Indian Urbanization Economist

Ambedkar wanted villages to become towns because of the caste system. Lenin also wanted urbanization. Mao made a planned effort to bring the villages into a unified unit as communes i.e. today's Zilla Parishads. Ambedkar thought in this context. Caste based professions are related to backward production system, karma, reincarnation and caste system theories support them so they do not develop and the society does not develop and Ambedkar felt that the caste system would be eradicated only when the marginal production system was removed.

It has been made clear in many ways that urban civilization and heavy industries bind people together. Ambedkar made it clear that the caste system was entrenched in the villages, and therefore Gandhi's word of rural swaraj was used to stabilize the power of the exploited castes. It is clear that Ambedkar's vision was very forward-looking if we look at the rise of Indian political leadership in the last sixty years from rural exploited castes. In rural swaraj, the dominant castes were elected as Sarpanches and then rose step by step to become chief ministers. Rural swaraj has prevented BC, SC and ST castes from rising as leaders from the village level.

Although Ambedkar was deeply saddened by the destruction of caste culture by the British, Ambedkar was passionate about the rural economy. Due to the caste system, this religious anger continued. Development of towns, cities, industries are thought to help in eradicating economic and social.inequalities Even more backward caste relations, social oppression and thus economic and political oppression can still be seen in the villages than in the towns. Ambedkar wished that it would be better if some villages were united to form a town.

8. Ambedkar as Indian Social Development Scientist

Ambedkar should be studied extensively with a comprehensive perspective. A comprehensive study of Ambedkar did not take place due to the fact that Ambedkar was not given the priority given to Gandhi and Nehru. The theories of Marxism were put forth and unaware of the Ambedkar's study of economics, they spent decades without even knowing they existed. A comparative study of Ambedkar's theories with the economic socio- political theories of Marx, Engels, Lenin, Mao, Gandhi and Nehru one would get a doubt whether there was any other national leader or any other leader except Ambedkar who cared about the Indian society in India and constantly pushed for its social development? Doubt that. Because there is no other Indian national leader who has seriously studied and written for the development of Indian society like Ambedkar. Short essays and speeches were promoted as grand theories about national leaders.Ambedkar achieved great heights as a true scientist of Indian social development.

As mentioned earlier, Ambedkar observed that economics is not an independent science by itself, it is constantly changing in the

Ambedkarism - Socialism

context of political, social, cultural and lifestyles. There is no such thing as eternal or fixed. Everything is changing. Ambedkar on one occasion made it clear that change is a characteristic of the individual as well as the society.

As Arthasastra describes the life activities of human beings, politics, culture, philosophy, caste professions, industrial sectors and religion were simultaneously concerned. Ambedkar examined Arthasastra in a comprehensive manner. He concluded through his works that Arthashastra cannot have a separate existence apart from these.

9. Ambedkar as an economist can change the Indian social system

Ambedkar worked throughout his life to change the Indian social order. He proposed abolition of caste to abolish the caste system. By clarifying caste as an investment, surplus wealth, surplus value, and that it is the center of power, Ambedkar also discussed caste as a part of economics. Buddhism has been practiced and shown to be another way to eradicate the caste system. He clarified that Hindu religion, Hindu culture, Mohammedan religion and Islamic culture are not suitable for democratic culture and Buddhist culture is the best way for it. Created the new Buddhist path. Thus Ambedkar became an economist, a sociologist and a man of the age who made proposals to radically change the social system in India.

10. Ambedkar as an economist concerned with the relation of religion, caste and ideology to economics.

Western economists, economists like Marx, Lenin, Mao etc. did not bother even they knew that there was a relationship between economics, religion, caste, ideology and social development. Moreover, religion is given the privilege of being a personal matter. Following that, Marxists in India, gave a privilege that caste is a personal matter like religion. So it means that those who are in power have been accepted as social leadership.

Feminists assert that all that is personal is social and political. However, they still ignore caste and religion as a social, political, economic and cultural problem. Ambedkar, unlike them, was a great economist who cared about all these. Thousands of pages of texts have been published against caste, religion, gender and ideology regarding the role they play in life. Marxists and Western economists still do not do this. Moreover, it was advertised that doing that would sidetrack the main points. In fact, Ambedkar kept clarifying that these were main points throughout his life.

Therefore, in modern times we do not find any Western or Eastern economists comparable to Ambedkar. Atheist rationalists and to some extent Marxists fought against religions and superstitions but their work could not be converted into a part of Arthasastra perspective like Ambedkar. It is for these reasons that Ambedkar does not seem to have any comparison or competition among the economists of the world.

11. Ambedkar who discussed economics as a social science as a social activist

Ambedkar is one of the great intellectuals of the world. However, his contribution as a social worker is immense. While working as a social worker to radically change the Indian society, he applied economics and discussed social, cultural, political, moral and ethical issues. Hence they have that special vocabulary and forms of science in diction. It is the task of today's economists to elucidate the underlying political economy of all of them.

Because while working as a social worker, Ambedkar did not give time or priority to write with regard to economics in the student stage. Ambedkar clarified that Political leadership alone was the master key to completely transform economical, political and social fields and was the only key to open the locks of all the issues. Thus, by extracting and codifying Ambedkar as an economist from all his writings, it becomes clear how Ambedkar as a social activist cared about economics throughout his life.

Ambedkar applied and analyzed Arthasastra in all spheres of life and social spheres. His efforts as a social philosopher also need to be codified when he is considered as an economist. Then Ambedkar appears as a social philosopher who analyzed economics through social sciences.

12. Ambedkar as Buddhist Economist

Ambedkar's Arthasastra is aptly termed as Buddhist arthashastra when his entire body of work is taken into account. In fact, Ambedkar's writings and sentiments have been recorded in such a vast way that it has been created as 'Ambedkarist Arthashastra'. Ambedkarist economics can also be called like Marxist economics, capitalist economics, democratic economics. Ambedkar adopted history, heritage, democratic principles and culture from the Buddha,

Ambedkarism - Socialism

unlike Kautilya's Arthashastra, which has continued throughout history, and when 'Ambedkarist Arthashastra' is considered as their legacy, Ambedkar Arthashastra can be termed as Buddhist Arthashastra and Ambedkar as Buddhist Arthashastra.

It can be said that it is within the scope of arthashastra to think that ideological understanding, propaganda and ideological struggle are more important than the use of force to eliminate inequalities. Some took over the kingdom through wars and armed conflicts. Ambedkar, in contrast, observed and practiced peaceful transformation, ideological conflict, mass consensus, propaganda war, etc. as contributing to fundamental changes.

Ricardo, Malthusius, Marx, Lenin, Stalin, Mao, Liantiev etc. had a different view of economics. People like Ambedkar had a different view of economics. Ambedkar's work as an economist can be classified as 'Buddhist Economics'.

Ambedkar's Buddhist Arthasastra (Buddhist Economy) was created as an antidote to these two Kautilya's Arthashastra, Manu's Anthropology.

Ambedkar conceived of an economics in which the social welfare of the people should be prioritized no matter who and which party was in power in a multi-party system in democratic process.

It is necessary to codify and synthesize the concepts of arthashastra contained in his writings to formulate Ambedkarist arthashastra and incorporate them in the textbooks. There are already some researches on this subject in other languages. It is known that they have emerged. The light brought by them needs to be widely disseminated.

B.S Ramulu

Pratitya Samutpada

Pratitya Samutpada means that many causes and motions come together to form another action, motion. It is popularly called causal relations. An action is done for a reason. It also means that one action causes another cause. Causality is a core element of dialectics in rationalism.

If Kant, Hegel, Marx and Engels had access to works on Pratitya Samutpada, they would have used the term Pratitya Samutpada instead of dialectics (Gatitarkam). The word dialectics is derived from the word dialogue. The phrase Pratitya Samutpada has been used since the beginning as a meaningful phrase about life, society, philosophy and logic. Pratitya Samutpada is somewhat broader than dialectics and comprehensive. Pratitya Samutpada has been explaining from the beginning that motions are interdependent. Everything is subject to change. If it existed, then it exists. Centuries ago, Buddhists explained about Pratitya Samutpada that if that perished, this would perish.

History is constructed by following the main causes in the construction of history. Some activities run like parallel lines and train tracks. While influencing each other and continuing separately, society and movements are driven forward. Like this Samutpada, along with causal theories, describes parallel lines of action in one coordination, synthesis, action, new causes, new developments in integrality. It understands. The analysis and solutions done in this way are called comprehensive social development and comprehensive social revolution. Each class, caste, region, language, country, gender, age, has a priority. A comprehensive social revolution is a movement to solve all of them simultaneously, and that is comprehensive social

Pratitya Samutpada

development. Modern governments, by taking care of all the problems of all classes, all ranks, the development of the society will be elevated comprehensively/

Kinetic materialism, historical materialism is limited to European developments. It is also not comprehensive. Primitive Commune, Slavery, Royal Feudalism, Capitalism, Proletariat, Socialist System are related to Europe. In other countries these consequences continued to take place specifically. Sharad Patil has extensively analyzed that there was no such thing as primitive commune system. Tribal Classes, patriarchal systems, Janapadas, emergence of kingdoms, empires, rural self-sustenance, economic and cultural life styles continued in the Indian subcontinent. Even in modern society, along with industrialization and computerization, casteism, tribal way of life, patriarchal family system and the culture treating the women as dependents continued simultaneously. Plans, procedures, budgets and administrative system have to be formulated to move all these from the backward stage to the modern stages in the five-year plans.

This perspective can be observed in the Constitution of India. This has been clearly stated in the Preamble and Fundamental Objectives of the Constitution of India. This is Pratitva Samutpada.

The main point is the relationship and conflict between the developed, the developing, and those who cannot receive development and power, and those who do not even know that they should receive them. Integral social development is the formulation and development of special procedures, programs and priorities to include all of them and grow equally with the developed ones. This is Pratitya Samutpada in democracy. In sociology, this is defined as working for social justice and social change in social philosophical, economic, cultural and literary fields against 'community, color, class, caste, gender, race, religion, region, country, language, discrimination and inequality' and is practiced. When he wrote the book 'Gatitarka Tatvadarshan Bhumika' in 1990, and in 1992 when he built the 'United Forum of Dalit (BC, SC, ST, Minority) Writers, Artists and Intellectuals', he declared this comprehensive social development and this philosophy as his plan.

History is the result of the movements of many factors. History is not just history of class struggles. Production forces, science, technology, administrative systems, constitutions, culture, blood relations, sentiments, religious concepts are the result of the movements of the activities of past history and present social developments. Some people think that conflict is the main thing in society. But contradictions do not arise without relation. Therefore, history is a collection of the consequences of the states of the relationship. Synthesis of all activities and analyzing chemical processes in a holistic manner and finding solutions is the sum total of all activities and is Pratitva Samutpada. Kinetic historical physics, kinetic physics were formulated by Marx and Engels following developments in Europe. Marx later recognized that the analysis of Marx's principles were limited to Europe. He undertook a new study of other regions, continents and countries. He also examined the caste problem. Indian leftists hide this matter.

Behind the formation of ideologies, culture, sentiments, human relations and blood relations in the society, there is a historical background, and there are many social, economic and cultural developments. Going further from the period of national movement, from the historical developments of the Mughal Empire, petty kingdoms, feudal systems, caste systems and varna systems, the European colonialists, modern inventions to modern industrial revolutions, production methods, societies, culture, sentiments, human relations, political system, strongly influenced theories. In that order, many theories and perspectives, old and new, conflicted with each other. Many social reforms, new ideologies, new ways of life, new methods of exploitation and new state administration systems came forward. Thus, in place of monarchies and royal dictatorships, democratic systems, working class dictatorship systems, mixed and economic policies have been taking shape. Following the human way of life, following the needs, and following the inevitability, their feelings; philosophies, theories, formulations, sentiments and blood relations are formed.

Indian society, as a modern society, from the industrial production system, from the colonial rule, from the monarchy, to the freedom movement, many ideologies and activities were brought forward. Many ideologies and movements advanced during the national movement.

Pratitya Samutpada

There are many historical developments behind India becoming what it is.

Rights of freedom and equality which are not experienced even though the Constitution provides for equal rights

Even though BC, SC, ST and minorities have been given equal rights and freedom in the Indian Constitution, they are unable to enjoy them fully due to family system, caste system, religious system and male dominance. Due to the feudal system, changes in the rural areas and implementation of the constitution became very difficult. Thus the majority of Hindus could not get their rights and equal freedom. Movements were necessary for the achievement of constitutional goals. The number of the movements started during the period of the national movement, began to decline after inde-pendence. Sectional Thinking. Their thought were confined to their category, their caste and their region. Made movements which lacked leadership that addressed the entire Indian race and Indian society. The respective parties were limited for their own power.

During the National Movement, RSS forces like Veera Savarkar propagated Hinduism. After independence they have expanded and taken many turns since the demolition of the Babri Masjid in 1992 in the name of Hindu religious supremacy, the upper caste and caste minority Hindus came to dominate the majority Hindus. The Muslim minorities are being bullied and the majority Hindus are being subjugated. Lohiyaism, Ambedkarism, Periyarism, M.N. Roy's radical humanism, leftism, trade unionism, Muslimism, the post-independence philosophy of Jiddu Krishnamurthy continued from the time of the national movement, and they spread it to whoever got the opportunity. Dravidian history, BC philosophy came forward in South India. BC Violent movement in Tamil Nadu took place under the leadership of Periyar after the High Court dismissed the case filed by Champakam Dorai Rajan on reservation. With that, a paragraph was added to the 14th article of the first amendment in the Constitution of India.

Lohiyaism advocates democratic socialism. Ambedkarism Dalitism advocates democratic socialism. Jiddu Krishna-murti's meditative work is detached from current issues. The Bahujans, the majority Hindus, and the caste based occupations were getting ruined, for the sake of livelihood, for the protection of caste based occupations and for subsidies they made movements. In this way, the majority of Hindus did movements similar to the national movement. But, their demands and goals were so small that they were not prominently recognized in the history of the national movement. Almost the same situation continued after independence. Since the 1980s, debates about the political power of BCs and SCs have picked up speed in the politics of ideologies and movements across the country. In fact BCs came to power in Uttar Pradesh and Bihar as early as 1967 with Lohiyaism. By 1967, Congress was defeated in half of the states and other parties came to power. DMK came to power in Tamil Nadu, CPM in Bengal and Lohia Socialist Party in Uttar Pradesh. In this way the power started to fall into the hands of the majority of Hindus. But, the minority Hindus came to power in the name of CPI and CPM and established themselves as dominant over the majority Hindus.

After independence, the spirit of national movement decreased and they moved separately for their own interests. In Telangana and Kerala in 1956, the Congress party prevented the Left parties from coming to power.

Serious inequalities in the formation of states

With the fall of the Mughal Empire and the expansion of British rule, the 565 provinces and the British-ruled areas different in size, population and culture continued in various ways. Their history, culture and mental unity were different. All these were reduced to 14 states following the recommendations of the Fazul Ali Commission for the redistribution of states.

The developed areas, backward areas, tribal areas, and rural areas, in the process of in-equal state formation, the dominant classes, castes, regions carried it out by way of internal colonialism and internal colonial rule. The discontents, inequality and repression intensified. After the formation of 14 states on November 1, 1956 with the 7th constitutional amendment, the main reason for many movements that took place in the country was due to the inequality behind the formation of states. Adivasi areas were demarcated to the respective states and advasis did not form their own states. As a result of many movements, 29 states and several Union Territories were formed. More than 15 separate states and movements are still going on. States

Pratitya Samutpada

like Uttar Pradesh, Bihar and Madhya Pradesh are the largest states and continue to dominate Indian politics. Movements are going on to form these into several states.

After independence, Congress, Lohia, Ambedkar, Periyar, Marxism, Gandhism, regionalism, humanism, made a strong impact in social, political and economic fields. The Swatantra Party run by people like Chakravarthula Rajagopalachari, NG Ranga were brought forward. People like Nastika Gora preached party less democracy. People like Pragada Kotaiah and Jogendranath Mandal brought forward many points in politics with the BC argument. He also stood and won in politics. A movement called Dalit Panthers came forward in Maharashtra in the year 1967. Naxalite movement started in Bengal. The Naxalites thought of an armed revolution. Simon Dibower gave a clarification to feminism by explaining the gaps and errors in Marxism through his book 'Second Sex'. Thus, many communists questioned the priorities and perspective of Marxism and invented new aspects. So all over the world, efforts were made for women's equality. Movements for reservation in legislatures continue. 1980 was declared by the United Nations as the Decade of Women. March 8 has been declared as Women's Day. On 7th August 1905, the Foreign Goods Boycott Movement began in Calcutta. Taking inspiration from it, the Government of India declared 7th August as Handloom Day. Such backward and oppressed social groups, castes and women need many procedures to get equality and move forward.

Telugu Nata In the 1970s, atheistic rationalist armed revolutionism, special Telangana and special Andhra views clashed in the society. Emergency was imposed on 25 June 1975 by Indira Gandhi. Emergency was lifted in February 1977 and elections were held. Then Indira Gandhi was defeated and Janata Party came to power. Morarji Desai became the Prime Minister. They were happy that the lost freedom had returned.

Since then many social reform movements have proliferated. Ideological consciousness and social movements have flown without barriers. The power of RSS and BJP also spread rapidly in the political field. RSS forces who shared power in the Janata Party got a taste of power. Those who were in the Jana Sangh joined the Janata Party after that they separated and formed their own party as Bharatiya Janata

Party and moved forward with their own agenda. Promoting Babri Masjid as Ram Janmabhoomi, L.K. Advani and others started Rath Yatras. The RSS and BJP forces, which underpin the varna and caste systems of their hegemony, in the name of patriotism have extended anti-Muslim and Brahminical Hindu ethos. RSS and BJP, which set out for the construction of a Hindu state with the religious fervor inherent in the majority of Hindus, were attracted to the sentiments, propaganda and politics of the BJP.

The sequence of pushing back BC reservations in the name of Hinduism

Although the Congress party continued in politics, later Bharatiya Janata Dal was formed and BJP joined it and returned to share in power. RSS, Vishwa Hindu Parishad has more than 70 branches. They went about their business. In 1980 B.P. Mandal's BC reservation report submitted during Indira Gandhi's tenure by V.P. Singh came out after ten years and proposed reservation in the field of employment. With that, the BJP withdrew its support to the government. V.P. Singh resigned. Kamandal, Ramjanma bhoomi and Rath Yatras were brought forward against the pro-Mandal Commission movement.

Feminism, Kansheeram, Bahujanism

On the other hand, the Bahujan Samaj Party was taking shape under Kanshiram's leadership. While the political field continued like this, feminism in the field of ideology and social movements, the Women's Decade came forward and spread all over the world. The armed movements spread. RSS spread the culture of Hindu philanthropy. Bahujana culture was born. Thus, the social and the fields of ideology have taken a turn. Atheist rationalism was weakened by that.

Kamma Caste into Power - NTR

Started in 1982 and in 1983 N.T. Rama Rao's Telugu Desam Party came to power. In 1981, police fired on a tribal assembly in Indravelli. In 1983, N.T. During Rama Rao's reign, there was a massacre of Dalits in Padarikuppam. Khali-stan Bindranwale movement started in 1984. After the assassination of Indira Gandhi in October 1984, the Sikhs were massacred. In 1985, there was a massacre by Karanchedu Kammavari. Dalit movements against this

Pratitya Samutpada

gained momentum. Bojja Tarakam, Kathi Padmarao, Usha S with the solidarity of several party movements. Under the leadership of Danny, Devulapalli Mastan Rao, Punnaiah and others, the Karanchedu Dalit movement moved forward. Despite their ideologies, they all worked together. With the Dalit Mahasabha movement gaining momentum, Ambedkarism once again came forward as a powerful ideology.

From RSS to Ambedkarism's Revolutionism

From 1960s to 1977, Ambedkarism, like the RSS, expanded its mission-oriented propaganda. After the Emergency of 1977, Ambedkar Yuvajan Sanghs etc. came into force all over the state. All of them merged with Karanchedu.movement. By then revolutionism and feminism were already firmly established. Combining them, Ambedkarism advanced, expressing dissent towards armed struggle. Feminists opposed patriarchy and also came together with the Dalit movement. Marxists and Leninists also came together with the leftist's ideology. Over the course of time, they clashed in society over whose views they held. Ideological discussions gathered a pace.

Having been RSS Chief Shikshak from 1967-72, I have been fascinated by Ambedkar's life, writings and sentiments since 1976. On one hand, while working with the Revolutionay Student Youth Associations and the Revolutionary Writers Associations, I moved forward by building the Ambedkar Youth Associations movements, organizing civil rights associations and job unions. As a member of Virasam since 1980, serving as the State General Secretary of the Radical Youth Association in 1984 and touring all India since 1985, I had many experiences. The breadth of feelings and understanding has increased. I have been participating in this conflict of ideologies verbally and in writing. I have written articles in weekly newspapers like Sunday Weekly. In support of the revolutionary movement, I wrote many stories including 'Batuku Nerpina Patham', 'Palu', 'Sahajatalu' and Badi. I discussed about feminism, about caste problem in India, coordinating with caste problems, writing articles in 'Aruntara' monthly and 'Udayam' daily under pen names.

Conflict between thought and practice - 1986

As part of that, I wrote an article on 'Contradiction between thought and practice'. Many people participated in the discussion along with the leaders of the revolutionary party for two years. Groups were formed here and there and debated for and against. Two ideological treatises were published earlier in the People's War Party. Proofreading and molding them worked well for me. Discussion started in the party on the issue of caste. Sivasagar named K.G. Satyamurthy, Gaddar,

B. S. Ramulu were deeply engrossed in discussions. At one stage Ganapati (Muppalla Lakshmana Rao) looked down on Ambedkar and Ambedkarism. We proposed to include Ambedkar and Ambedkarism in the caste problem as Mao included Sun et Sign in China. I discussed why Ambedkarism which solves the caste problem should not be included when womenism is included. It was strongly opposed. They thought that there should be a discussion on this matter in the party. They asked me to write what I thought and they would discuss. I wrote it. They said that they did not not understand this. They refused to elaborate and distribute because they said they did not understand it and how could they distribute it to the cadre.

Discussions in the People's Party

In the People's Party, there were many verbal discussions on the issue of caste, armed revolution and the procedures of the public associations in the state and in the public associations. There were discussions about Ambedkar, Buddhist philosophy about the caste problem. It was also seriously discussed that there is a need to get rid of constraints in the strategic moves programs and create procedures that work freely and peacefully among the people. After a serious discussion on the caste issue, a challenge was made whether I would switch my side towards them or they would switch their side towards my side.

The upper castes come for leadership

In any organization, in any movement, upper castes and upper castes come and work for leadership. They cannot tolerate working as activists. They don't really like working under the leadership of BC, SC, ST. Accepting their leadership, dominance, and working under their leadership can be like emotionally stung by snakes, scorpions, and red ants. Their caste-based ideology continued changing their body language and their feelings and personality that way.

All the negotiations to solve the caste problem and remove the upper caste rule, and to let the oppressed working class to take the lead

Pratitya Samutpada

in policy- making positions, the caste problem, the women problem, the class problem, Mahatma Jyotiba Phule, Dr. B.R. Ambedkar were being neglected, denied, oppressed, distorted by the upper class continued to establish their supremacy. All this with the understanding of many movements, political developments, the evolution of ideologies, and having studied history, I have consistently maintained the conflict of ideologies.

The evolution of ideology since 1990 around the world

The collapse of Soviet Russia, glasnost perestroika GAT deals, globalization, privatization, liberalization, ideologies and politics gathered pace. In the party and in public life, it was openly discussed that if the issue of caste is not taken care of in the public and in the literature, the supremacy of the elite will continue even in the revolutionary parties. In Premchand's novel 'Rangabhoomi' written in 1912, I explained as an example how the upper caste revolutionary became anti-movement and anti-people when he lost his dominance in the movement. They said that it is not right for me to continue in the party and the movement after such a serious discussion. They said that I should limit myself to literature and write stories and novels. It was very painful to hear such words after leaving the government job and family to join the Movement. I have discussed in newspapers under pen names. They asked me not to write even if I write with pen names, as my language, sense and style would be known. It is a tragedy to go from turning life around for feelings to being exposed for feelings.

Into public life in April 1990

Finally time came together and in 1989 Dr. After Marri Chenna Reddy became the Chief Minister again in April 1990, I came into public life in the District Mahasabha of the Radical Youth Association held in Manthani in collaboration with Duddilla Sripadarao. That same night, Gaddar, Varavara Rao, Devulapalli Amar, Mabhumi Sandhya, Ganji Rama Rao and others left together in a jeep and handed me over to Shyamala at my home in Jagitiyala, saying, "Here is your husband." So when I came into public life in April 1990, as promised by the then Chief Minister Marri Chenna Reddy, I was immediately given my old job by the Collector. I had to give in writing that from that day onwards, I would not participate in direct politics and would limit myself to social, cultural and literary movements.

However, many times, even after that, I faced restrictions. That is another step.

Winged feelings

Coming into public life gave me the freedom and opportunity to fully express my feelings. Soviet Russia split into 13 countries. Leftist ideology has been the subject of many debates around the world. The views of Gramsci, Georgi Lucas, Rosa Luxemburg, Che Guevara, Trotsky, Bukharin are again discussed with emphasis. Against this backdrop, I toured the entire state propagating my views on the caste problem, class perspective and the revolutionary movement. The old ones are gone. The newcomers came close. The documents I wrote for the party were published serially in the Dalit Voice magazine after editing and reformulating them. With that, a new readership like me has been formed. In that order, I have gone ahead to unite all BC, SC, ST and minority writers so that all those who are working somewhere can become one. Katti Padmarao defined the term Dalit as an inclusive term.

We have named the organization 'United Forum of Dalit Writers, Artists and Intellectuals'. In June 1992, those who met at the Dalit Literature Conference in Utnur prepared a pamphlet and sent it to magazines, writers and artists. It went on under the leadership of Guda Anjaiah. At the state level, a conference on Dalit literature was held at Karimnagar on December 6, 1992. On the same day, Babri Masjid was demolished in Ayodhya in Uttar Pradesh. An alert was announced across the country. However we changed the venue and held the conference till midnight at the Upadhyaya Sangam office in Mankammathota, Karimnagar. The next day we released statements condemning the Babri Masjid demolition.

Darakame Aikya Vedika State Mahasabhas

Darakame Aikya Vedika' meetings were held in Warangal, Hyderabad, Kurnool and other districts and on 13-14 February 1993, we organized the first state conference of 'Dalit Writers, Artists, Intellectuals Aikayavedika' at Ambedkar Bhavan under Tank Bund in Hyderabad. More than 2 thousand writers, artists, intellectuals and fans attended. By that time, the Bahujan Samajwadi Party was also resurgent and the Chundur Dalit movement was moving across the country in 1991. B.R. Ambedkar Sata Jayanti Sabhas were held, movements took place in favor and against the implementation of the

Pratitya Samutpada

Mandal Commission, P.V. Narasimha Rao became the Prime Minister and promoted globalization, privatization and liberalization. BCs, SCs and STs mobilized everywhere against privatisation. We have been synthesizing the need for feminism, Ambedkarism, Mandalism, Ambedkarism, Buddhism.

U. Sambasiva Rao, Kanche Ailaiah, Rama Rao

In their way since 1986, working on these mattersSambasivarao Kanche Ailaiah and others met with us. Masterji, who has been working with the Dalit Art Council since 1978, has been promoting Ambedkarism. Naragoni, who came forward in the pro- mandal movement, got involved with the ideology of the Bahujan Samaj Party. On the other hand, Ingilala Ramachandra Rao, Rajasekhar from Nellore, Durgam Subba-rao from Guntur, B.M. Kadar Mohiuddin from Leelakumari, Vijayawada, Punugoti Krupakar Madiga from Prakasam district, Kadali Satyanarayana Bodhi of Godavari Keratal from Kakinada, K. Seetharamulu, Jupalli Satyanarayana from Khammam; Professor Jaya Saloni, Nanamasa Swamy from Hyderabad; Anishetti Rajitha from Warangal, P.N. Speaker, P. Rams; K. Ramalakshman, Tulsi Sampath from Karimnagar; Adilabad to Guda Anjaiah, G.R. Kurme, P.C. Ramulu, Dr. Damera Ramulu and others came together from across the state. Meetings were held everywhere.

Maroju Viranna, Daphodam

Maroju Veeranna has already discussed in his movement party and came out on the issue of caste. He undertook to organize the caste societies with a new spirit. To cope with this, Kura Rajanna, on behalf of Vimochana group, held state conferences on the caste problem in Rayalaseema. We all participated in it. They later set up 'Dafodom' in Guntur parallel to us. It was with some dissatisfaction that I worked with this competing organisation. The organisation did not move forward.

Darakame Aykya Vedika, Expanded

We penetrated across the state in the process of songs, poems, lectures, theory study classes etc. At that time conferences on Telugu story novel were organized in Anantapur. I attended them. There, Shantinarayana, Bandi Narayanaswamy, Dr. Kolkaluri Inak, Dr. K. Lakshminarayana came into contact. 'Dalit Writers,Artists and Intellectuals' State Congress with Nastika Ramakrishna, Kathi

B.S Ramulu

Padmarao, Bojja Tarakam, Bojja Vijayabharathi, M. B.N. (Nizamabad) Boya Jangaiah, K.S. Chalam, Nanamasa Swamy, Prabhanjan, Gali Vinod Kumar, Visakha to Kondapalli Sudarshan Raju, Y. Satyanarayana, Madishetti Tirumala Kumar, Vijayalakshmi from Vijayawada, all our ideologies became a great stream. This decade has been declared ours. If the 1970s were the decade of men, the

1980s were the decade of women. We have declared 1990 as Dalit Bahujan decade. Daraka was the turning point brought by the united platform.

We declare that 'Darakame Aikyavedika' is a great turning point in the history of literature spanning thousands of years from Nannayya to today. We owned Joshua. We rejected Sri Sri and Viswanatha Satyanarayana. Thus the speed of the conflict in the consciousness of ideology increased. We had serious discussions on Gurjada Apparao, Chalam and Srisri from the perspective of Ambedkarism. Essays on Chalam, Sri Sri by Qader Mohiuddin, B.S. Ramulu's essay on Gurajada as "How to look at Kanya Shulkam today" created a great sensation in the fields of literature and philosophy. There were endless debates in various daily and weekly magazines.

Text poetry collections

In that order, G. Lakshminarsayya and Juluri Gauri Shankar together with Dalit text poetry wrote, the song titled Chikkanavutunna Pata, Padunekkina Pata and got it printed as textual poetry. When Juluri Gowrishankar organised Dalit Literary Conference in Nalgonda district we all supported and participated. We brought a few issues of the monthly magazine 'Gabbalam'. Many who remained neutral from the textual poetry and had an inherently leftist outlook evolved into Ambedkar's perspective. Endluri Sudhakar and Satish Chander are the main ones. G. Laxminarsayya discussed about Ambedkarism and Marxism, Indian Marxism is Ambedkarism. Raised some yard work. Bojja Vijayabharati has written many works with the perspective of Ambedkarism. They are published by the Hyderabad Book Trustees. Ranganayakamma, who was associated with feminism and morphism, should have supported BC and SC. But worked against it. At the same time, many women writers like Volga, Rama Egte, Lalitha, Sajaya supported Darakameka's united platform and Dalitism.

Pratitya Samutpada

BCs and Women in Legislature

Movements to introduce reservations for BCs and women in legislatures came forward. We hoped to see these two groups cooperate with each other. But, the feminists moved forward separately. More importantly, while the RSS and BJP Hindu fundamentalists are expanding on the one hand, feminists across the country have remained largely silent instead of working extensively in the ideological,, philosophical, cultural and literary fields against Hinduism, against the varna, caste, caste system and patriarchal system it promoted. If the feminists had marched together with BC, SC and ST against the patriarchal system, Hindu communa-lism would not have spread so much. Pluralism, Hinduism of the majority would have advanced stronger and stronger.

Threat brought in by disunity - disintegration

By working together like this, and later on, as the respective movements working separately, the Hindutva forces integrated into a single organization gained strength day by day. The main reasons for that are the neglect of the need for unity of other parties in the political sphere, social, philosophical and literary spheres. Finally, the atheist rationalisms that did not support BC, SC, ST were watered down. They almost became difficult to locate. In this way, some forces in the society moved forward unitedly, while other forces moved forward disunitedly, in the political arena, UPA was formed under the leadership of Congress, while NDA was formed under the leadership of BJP. In between, federal structures such as the Janata Dal, formed by Lohia's socialists with democrats, crumbled. Broke up. Although the respective regional parties and regional ideologies are trying to form a federal front from time to time, they are not moving forward together in the fields of literature, philosophy and culture. These theoretical discussions were conducted by Dr. SV Satyanarayana has recorded the history of feminism debates and dalitism debates by publishing separate books. Kondalarao brought out a collection of essays titled BC Mitrulu. Vinu-konda Bhaskar Rao, Justice B.S. Swami jointly organized a magazine called Manapatrika for a few years. From Kaki Madhavrao, to Kanche Ailaiah, B.S. Ramulu, Kathi Padmarao and many others contributed towards it.

Contribution of Darakame Aikya Vedika

B.S Ramulu

'Gatitarka Tatvadarshan Bhumika' wrote by B.S.Ramulu, book 'Why I am not Hindu' by Kanche Ailaiah, 'Mulavasi Siddhanta' by Mastarji, 'Ambedkarism Marxism - Philosophical Discussions' by Ingilala Ramachandra Rao, V.G.R. Naragoni's 'Bahujanavada Siddhanta', hundreds of songs, thousands of works, Daraka is the greatest contribution of Aikyavedika. Standing on its own in the field of philosophy, Ikyavedi has established its own philosophical position. Thus, in 1993, they announced their plan by synthesizing all the arguments that Daraka would work unitedly in the social, literary and philosophical fields against the discrimination and inequalities of the community, color, class, caste, gender, race, religion, region, country and language. It is a broader, broader perspective, adopting the legacy of Buddhism, Ambedkarism, and Phuleism as a foundation.

1980-90 was a decade of ideological conflicts

Between 1980-90s RSS, Hindu religious forces, democratic forces, BC reservation groups, Bahujan Samajwadi Party ideology, revolutionary party ideology, Dalitism, feminism etc. were in constant conflict. The train tracks are opposite and never meet. But the train runs on them. Earlier it was said that a cart could move only if its wheels are parallel. Railroads are a more obvious comparison. Different feelings, social actions, movements and practices run like railroad tracks in society. The train of society moves forward over them. Since 1980, some trains have been moving forward in philosophical, social, cultural and literary fields. In the 1980s, feminism came up on the one side of the tracks. Humanism, Socialism, Equality, Freedom and Constitution of India were already running on the tracks. Dalit pluralism came forward from 1985 along with feminism. It questioned the caste system and the discrimination and inequality in it. Since 1990, feminism and Dalitism have gone hand in hand. On the other hand, the philosophy, practice and movements of Marxism have been progressing.

Deep discussions were held in the respective parties on caste problem, women problem, Dalit problem, BC problem, minority problem etc. The conflict escalated. Many groups were formed. Following one's experience and understanding, they advanced by adding new applications to the old ones. Upper Caste minority Hindus were ahead of others in making new applications of the old. The new proposals faced several obstacles. Not many could give up on the old

Pratitya Samutpada

applications. Even in Marxism, new interpretations and new applications of the old ones have been published.

Gatitarka Tatvadarsana Bhumika - 1990

Since 1985, after the Karanchedu incident, there have been many debates in ideologies and movements. Later BSP came forward. Discussions were held internally in the respective industries. On their own, all of them later printed the documents written in the internal discussions. So I edited and revised the documents written since 1985 into a book. I brought a book called 'Gatitarka Tatvadarsana Bhumika'. It was first serialized in 'Dalit Voice' magazine. The first edition was published as a book in 1991. I printed only 250 copies and sent them to famous social activists, literary men and philosophers in Telugu. Ranganayakamma wrote a small letter. After that she wrote a book "Buddha is not enough, Ambedkar is not enough, Marx is enough". The essence of this is Buddha, Ambedkar are not wanted, and concluded that Marxism alone is enough. She named it differently. Inspired by the book 'Gatitarka Tatvadarsana Bhumika', CPI organized a seminar on 'Caste Problem in India' in Vijayawada. I gave a keynote speech there.

'Buddhism, Socialism, Ambedkarism'

Since 1993, I have written articles titled 'Buddhism, Socia-lism, Ambedkarism' and published it as a book. K. Balagopal's book said that he would write a review on 'Gatitarka Tatva-darshana Bhumika' after reading it. He said that the whole thing is not favorable, but he will discuss some things. He changed his mind, for the reasons unknown, and he discussed about the novel 'Rago' with man and nature. That discussion went on for two years across the state. The respective parties have set up special departments for women and special departments for caste issues. Changes and additions have been made in this way. Thus Karanchedu and Chundur Bahujan Samajwadi Party movements 'Darakame Aikya Vedika' concerted effort accelerated the evolution of Telugu based ideologies from 1990 onwards. That's why we have the 1970-80 decade as the vexation decade. But while 1980-90 was the decade of women, 1990-2000 was the decade of Dalit Bahujan. In 1992, after the formation of the Dalit Bahujan writers, artists and intellectuals, many changes took place in the society, literature and philosophical understanding. All this is the result of efforts of Dalit Bahujan organizations and literati.

B.S Ramulu

Ninety percent of those who think they know Marxism do not know the origins of Marxism. They remained traditionalists in Marxism. Naturally, most of them are minority Hindus who come from varna dominated and caste-dominated communities. In other words, they resorted to Marxism to maintain their supremacy. In the form of Marxism, caste and caste supremacy is being continued. For that, they use Marxist words and quotes and scare the common people. Many have done this work. The fundamentals of Marxism are left out and discussed superficially. They emphasize about their strategy, moves and action plan. Like this in the discussion of ideologies and philosophical discussions, many points have come forward. No one dares to record this history. Everyone of them kept away the discussions of others and started writing and talking about themselves. Very few people spoke about this effort and the consequences in many national seminars.

They wrote hundreds of pages about digambara of poets who wrote for 5 years in literature. They could not ignore caste discrimination and caste oppression in the country and life. All of them were subject to upper caste restrictions. Apart from Dwana Shastri, no other literati could write about the united efforts of these Dalit Bahujan literati, Dalit Bahujan writers and intellectuals. In recording the evolution of literary history and the evolution of philosophical history, this discrimination and oppression continues. This is nothing new to society. They pretended as if they did not read the work of people like Mahatma Jyoti Rao Phule, Savitribhai Phule, Gadge Na Periyar Ramaswamy Naykar, Hayatidas, Dr. B.R. Ambedkar and the syntheses they brought. From D.D. Kosambi to Kallur Bhaskaram, who recently wrote a book on the Mahabharata, these philosophical and social developments were put aside as untouchable. In this way, in philosophical ideologies and movements, are running like two railway tracks in parallel. Without these two rails, the train of society cannot move forward. But those who say these two things with equanimity help the society to move forward with equanimity. This was lacking.

Buddhism, Marxism, Ambedkarism, Feminism, Subaltern Truth, Regional Existentialisms, etc., all can be seen to be synthesized and harmonized in the Constitution of India. In a multi-party system, the objective of the constitution of India is to peacefully continue

Pratitya Samutpada

Socialism, social justice, and social change. It is the fundamental objective of the Constitution of India and Ambedkarism to eliminate the gap between the privileged to be leading in power and development, and the underprivileged. It is the fundamental objectives of the constitution. Male dominated socialism is a women's problem. Feminism came forward. Varna system and caste systems were formed due to patriarchal hegemony. Therefore the varna and caste systems are the source of women's problem. Thus, removing the patriarchal dominance, equality, dignity, freedom and self-respect were proposed.

'Gatitarka Tatvadarsana Bhumika' was published in 1991. In 1998, a comprehensive third edition of several essays was published. 'Gatitarkam Ambedkarism, Marxism' in 1993, 'Ambedkarism Socialism' in 1996, 'What is Love?', 'Flowing Song' Dalit Songs of Andhra Pradesh, 'Materialism as a Worldview', 'Birth of Knowledge' in 1998, 'Pluralism' in 2003, 'What to do for B.C. , What BCs Should Do', '60 Years of Philosophical Social Development', 'Sovereignty for BCs', 2009 'What is Social Justice?' I published other books. In the field of ideology, they played their role in social movements. At the same time, 42 books were published as part of the Telangana state movement. In 2008, a book serialized in our magazine and published as a book, 'Shudras are the makers of Indian history', the history that the majority Hindus have contributed to the society over the centuries was described. I have been writing and publishing books from time to time on history, philosophy, literary theories and social movements. In addition to that I have also added the Telangana aspect. As mentioned in the 'United Forum of Dalit Writers, Artists and Intellectuals' in 1992, it is 'simultaneous work against discrimination and inequality of caste, gender, race, religion, country, region and language' and to work towards community building by writing hundreds of articles, books and to publish them. It is a parallel literary, social and historical development. It is a collective observation and analysis.

After the establishment of Darakame Aikya Vedika, the district-level katha, song, theory and discourse training workshops were organized for the young budding writers and artists of the day, and the social ideology was propagated widely. Authors, poets and artists were given direction. Those who wrote without any ambition or aim were given shown a way. It also reminded some of the elite writers and intellectuals of their responsibilities by turning their attention towards social ideology. 'Daraka is a united platform'. That is why some people supported 'Darakame Aikya Vedika'. Ambedkar Dharmaporata Samiti was started on December 25, 1995 in Nellore district under the leadership of Ingilala Rama Chandrayya Bodhi, a philosopher of Darakame Aikya Vedika. Calling upper castes as Arei, Orei, Turei continued as a movement against the calls of upper castes, Arei, Orei, Osei for social equality. Even though many cases were filed, there was a lot of change in the district.

From the spirit of 'Darakame Aikya Vediki', BCism and Minorityism developed into separate branches and separate movements. Feminism and feminist movements continued separately. Thus many social reform movements continued to split. All these need to be united in one unified event. Only then will they grow as a formidable force in political, social, economic and cultural fields. They come to power and development. Their empowerment will advance in all fields. Nastika Ramakrishna, Kathi Padmarao, Professor K.S. Chalam etc. for social reforms, egalitarian ideologies restudied and reconstructed history, issues, regions, ancient literature for dissemination.

Through 'Darakame Vedika' we have made efforts to build a united organization across the country. Heads of several states have been contacted. We discussed with people like Sharada Patil and Gail Omvid from Maharashtra. Sharad Patil said that caste is the main contradiction in the country and wants to spread the movement of Ambedkarism and Marxism across the country. Gail Omvid has given several talks on the synthesis of Ambedkarism, Marxism and Dalitism. Works and books were published. We thought it was not sufficient.

We have built a comprehensive social, philosophical, cultural and literary perspective against all, colour, class, caste, gender, race, religion, region, countryand language discriminations and inequalities. We have proposed this as compre-hensive social revolution and comprehensive social. Development. Thus the need for the innovation of social reforms was brought forward in all fields simultaneously. Thus, the subaltern movements and perspectives going on in the world today by including democratic socialism and

Pratitya Samutpada

peaceful transitions and moving forward. This synthesis takes the legacy from Buddha to Pule, Ambedkar with a vision of comprehensive social development and puts forward how should it be achieved in a multi-party system for democratic socialism. A serious effort was made to spread this view in all parties.

Today BJP, RSS, minority Hindus are dominating the majority Hindus. This is a development due to the disunity of the majority Hindus. What the minority Hindus want is a phase where the majority Hindus are divided.

Majority Hindus, in the light of the Constitution of India, with minimum program agreements for comprehensive social development, learning from the formation failures of Janata Party and Janata Dal should build more comprehensive federal national level single events and parties. The majority of Hindus will come to power in the political, economic and cultural fields only when the intellectuals in the literary, cultural, economic and social fields overcome their limitations and transcend the existential boundaries to provide leadership to the community and the nation. For that, like Kanshiram, the aspirations, ideologies, culture and sentiments of all regions, castes and communities should be taken forward. It is not far away if we get rid of individual egos and work collectively, the majority Hindus will come to power in the states. Janata Party and Janata Dal have proved how soon majority Hindus will come to power if all come together.

Profile of the Author

B.S. Ramulu was the First Chairman, Telangana State Commission for Backward Classes

Shri B.S. Ramulu, who is appointed as Chairman of the Commission that is constituted for the first time by Telangana Government for Backward Classes, is a well-known Social Philosopher, Maha Mahopadhyaya, Katha Samrat, Social Scientist and multi-talented personality. He is the writer who gave philosophical touch to Telugu short story. Though the theme of his literary works revolves specifically around the life in Telangana, Mr. Ramulu has carved a niche among those eminent philosophers who are committed to unveiling the conscience of our nation and chronicling the social, economic history of Indian society.

He has vast experience and practical knowledge acquired through study and struggle of life which enabled him to formulate new ideas about the long-debated issues such as Caste structure, Caste discrimination and place of Women. Mr.Ramulu has been writing relentlessly on various social and political issues for the last 3 decades. Many cultural organizations and political parties have taken their cue from his writings. So far he has 450 published articles to his credit.

BS Ramulu was born on 23-08-1949 in Jagityal, Jagityal district. His father late Sri Mittapalli Narayana was a worker in a cloth mill in Mumbai, his mother late Smt. Bethi Laxmirajam was a worker in a beedi factory. His parents belong to Padmashali (weavers) community. When BS Ramulu was 6 years old his father died and he was raised by his mother.

In the 60's Mr.Ramulu took active role in a number of social, literary and cultural movements. Encouraged by the ripened experience and knowledge he attempted to integrate/synthesize the common elements of Minoritism, Feminism, Humanism and Bahujanism (BC, ST, SC ideology) since 1990. As a senior writer who wrote more than 175 short stories and 7 novels Mr. Ramulu has conducted Writer's Workshops to offer guidance to amateur writers many of whom have become established writers now. He published two important books entitled "Kathala Badi" and "Katha Sahitya Alankara Shastram" for the benefit of writers of new generation. As a memorial of his mother late Smt. Mittapalli Laxmiraju (1930 to 1991) he has founded "Vishala Sahiti - BS Ramulu Katha Puraskaralu" and has been giving awards to writers from his 50th birth (golden jubilee) anniversary onwards.

Short Stories and Novels:

Bathukuporu Novel (3rd reprint-2004) (1982, Paalu (1991), Smruthi (1997), Mamatalu-Manava Sambandhalu (2000), Vepachettu (2003), Tenetigalu (2004), Paalu - Itara Kathalu (2004), batukupayanam (2005), Kaalam Techina Maarpu (2013), Chicagolo Nanamma (2013), Geluchukunna Jivitam (2013), Journey of Life (English) (2013), Struggle of Life (English) (2013), Values (English) (2014), Chupu (Novel) (2014) (2014), Aadavilo Vennala Kathala Samputi (2015), Illu-Vakili Kathal Samputi (2015). As a part of the Telangana movement 40 books regarding history and culture. Compiled and published books of songs with 1200 lyrics... Vishala Sahiti BC, SC, ST songs... Vishala Sahiti Children's songs and other anthologies... And also 250 stories as anthologies published. Published more than 80 books on various themes under his editorship. 50 of his stories published in various collection of books. He was honoured more than 250 well known, and upcoming writers with "Vishala Sahiti B.S. Ramulu Story Awards". In 1991 B.S. Ramulu published 'Gatitarka Tathva Darshana Bhumika (Philosophy and Dialectical Philosophy). That book gave a new direction to the ideological debate in the Telugu speaking state. It laid foundation for

B.S Ramulu

formation of BCs, SCs, and STs United Forum of Writers, Artists and Intellectuals (DARAKAME) Since 1992 B.S. Ramulu is the Founder President of 'A.P. United Forum of Dalit Writers, Artistes and Intellectuals' B.S. Ramulu also strived for the cause of women.

Some of his theoretical writings: 'Gnanam Puttuka', 'Prema Ante Emiti?', 'Pata Puttuka', Samskrutika Udyamalu', "BClu Sadhikarikatha', 'Kotha Charitra', 'Aravayyela Tathvika , Samajika Parinamalu', 'Mee Vurini Mere Aadhyanam Cheyyandi'... etc. He wrote prefaces and reviews to over 225 books. He toured the country and gave many philosophical speeches. "In the ideological revolution and ideological debate that have been taking place in Telugu speaking contribution of B.S. Ramulu weighs on the others, in the scale..." 10 books including 6 M.Phils, One Ph.D. published on his life & mission. And researches are going.

Awards and Recognitions:
1. Kodavatiganti Kutumba Rao award - 1984,
2. Dasarathi Rangacharya award for 'Batuku Poru' Novel - 1992
3. Former Minister, Freedom Fighter, Leader of BC movements Konda Lakshman Bapuji Foundation award.
4. Telugu University Endowment award in the name of Rationalist Tripuraneni Ramaswamy Choudary - 1995.
5. Telugu University Best Story Collection award for anthology Mamtalu Manava Sambandhalu 2002.
6. mahatma Jyotiba Phule Fellowship 2001 by Dalit Sahitya Academy, Delhi.
7. Rama Vriksha Benipuri Centanary award Panipat, Haryana.
8. First ever Yashoda Reddy memorial award and golden bracelet 2008.
9. First ever Telangana State formation award by Telangana Saraswata Parishat 2016.

The Active Role of Mr. Ramulu during Telangana Movement:
Mr.Ramulu has been playing an active role in Telangana Movement since 1995. In 2003 he resolved to dedicate his entire time for this cause. In pursuance of his goal he declared that he would

publish a book every month to show the path to be taken by the Movement from time to time. In his books he also tried to critically review and record the pace of the Movement.

Telangana Talli was designed in 2007 and dedicated to Telangana people. During "Telangana Sambaralu" program which was held in March 2007 in Nizam college premises. B.S. Ramulu was felicitated and offered 'Bangaru Kadiyam '(Golden Bracelet) as the designer of Telangana Talli by Sri K.Chandra Shekar Rao. B.S. Ramulu won so many accolades for literature. He is a perennial river of innovative thoughts and Indian philosophical consciousness. He is a walking school of short stories and a vital source of inspiration.

He encouraged inter caste and inter religious marriages. He campaigned to ignite the spirit of democracy, socialism and social reforms in various organizations. He took active part in social forums that work for elimination of caste and is opposed to caste and gender discrimination. He is a strong proponent of modern education for all. He strived for poor people to enable them to get food, cloth and shelter on par with others; In one word, B.S. Ramulu's contribution in the field of social reforms is multi-faceted.

KASTURI VIJAYAM

00-91 95150 54998
KASTURIVIJAYAM@GMAIL.COM

SUPPORTS

- PUBLISH YOUR BOOK AS YOUR OWN PUBLISHER.

- PAPERBACK & E-BOOK SELF-PUBLISHING

- SUPPORT PRINT ON-DEMAND.

- YOUR PRINTED BOOKS AVAILABLE AROUND THE WORLD.

- EASY TO MANAGE YOUR BOOK'S LOGISTICS AND TRACK YOUR REPORTING.

www.ingramcontent.com/pod-product-compliance
Lightning Source LLC
LaVergne TN
LVHW032011070526
838202LV00059B/6402